Flin Flon
A
Visual History
1933-1983

Researched and Compiled by
Stephanie Jarvis, Lois Burke
and Joyce Henderson
1983

Acknowledgements

Our purpose in setting down a visual history of Flin Flon originally was to provide a remembrance for our Jubilee Year. A book that would perhaps complement the written history book published by the Flin Flon Historical Society in 1974.

It was in the doing this that it became more than a project and a part of our lives.

We would like to thank the citizens of Flin Flon, past and present, some of whom are contained within the pages of this book, without whom there wouldn't have been a visual history.

Our thanks to the city of Flin Flon for giving us the opportunity to work on this project, the Flin Flon Historical Society, Flin Flon Public Library and the Hudson Bay Mining & Smelting Co., Limited. This record would have been impossible without the co-operation of many individuals who selected photos from their collections and answered innumerable questions.

Special thanks to Bruce and Darlene Reid, Rich Billy, Tom Dobson and Reuben Hagan for providing photos, advice and making our jobs so much easier and enjoyable.

We gratefully acknowledge the patience and understanding of our families and friends. It was a long year.

Our apologies to any we may have inadvertently left out.

ISBN 0-88925-439-7

Published by
Flin Flon Jubilee Committee
Flin Flon, Manitoba, R8A 0M8
Canada

First printing, 1983

Printed and bound in Canada by
Friesen Printers
a Division of D. W. Friesen & Sons Ltd.
Altona, Manitoba R0G 0B0
Canada

OUR TOWN

It's boulevards are barren rock
With patches here and there
Of Polular stumps and rounded lumps
Of muskeg, brown and bare.

It's little shacks and houses
Are every shape and size,
Some way down in the muskeg brown
And some up in the skies.

A mill, some shops, a hoistroom,
A headframe out of line,
An assay lab and a bunkhouse drab
And a dump, make up the mine.

The motley population,
Has come from East and West
Alsase-Lorraine and rich Ukraine
Hong Kong and Budapest.

Spaghetti-eating 'Talians,
And garlic-eating Jews,
Yonsons tight and Finn's who fight
And Scotsmen chasing booze.

The streets are never empty,
The cafes never close
There's mirth and song the whole day long
From blanant radios

The parlour seems like bedlam
With raucous shouts and roars,
While lusty calls and sounds of brawls
Float through the pool room doors.

But yet, with all it's ups and downs
I do not sulk or frown,
If the price of Gold will only hold
It's God's own very town.

— Author Unknown

The above poem was found in a local newspaper, circa 1934-39.

This, then, was our beginning.

The people that came to Flin Flon were from varied economic and cultural backgrounds. Not satisfied to relinquish a part of their past lifestyles, and surrounded by rock, trees and water, they melded their efforts together to form a solid community, despite their isolation. And so, aided and encouraged by the Mining Company, they learned to work and play together.

Much has been written and said about Flin Flon and these people who came only to seek their fortunes, but stayed to build a community; about smelter smoke and sewer boxes, harsh winters and hockey players, exporting children to higher learning along with the copper, about what makes Flin Flon unique. The uniqueness of Flin Flon cannot be captured by picture or the written word. It came from the hearts of those men and women who came North, never asking who a man was, but what he could do. A uniqueness that breeds people with warm hearts and willing hands. Over the years all men have remained, one with another. It is this feeling that makes Flin Floners, wherever they go, group together.

The Jubilee Committee have endeavored to recapture some of the comraderie of our parents and grandparents during the events of this Anniversary year. The Editors of this book have attempted to depict the working, cultural and recreational aspects of life in Flin Flon over some fifty years. As you peruse these pages may you recall many happy occasions of life here. This Visual History could not have been completed without the generosity of so many people who donated of their moment in time that we may enjoy. This book is dedicated to all those who have, who are and who will live in Flin Flon. This will always be a community more precious than the metals it exports.

Delores Baird
1983 Jubilee Chairman

Flin Flon Camp 1917. (Geological Survey of Canada)

Left to right — Tom Creighton, Leon Dion, Dan Mosher, John Mosher and Jack Hammell — 1917. (Flin Flon Archives)

The MANDY MINE "Glory Hole" at Schist Lake winter of 1916-1917.

High grade copper ore was hauled by horse team during the winter months from Mandy Mine to Sturgeon Landing and stock-piled for delivery to The Pas in the summer. (Manitoba Archives)

Then dumped manually into the barge. (Manitoba Archives)

The ore was loaded from the stockpile into buggies — (Manitoba Archives)

The barges were pushed by boat (S. S. Nipawin) to The Pas. The ore was then loaded into boxcars and shipped to the Smelter at Trail, B.C. Approximately 26,000 tons of ore was shipped from 1917 to 1920. (Manitoba Archives)

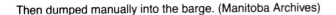

Flin Flon property September 1920. Wharf and ice house on the edge of the lake, office — centre, bunkhouses to the right.

The Manitoba Legislative Assembly travelled north in the fall of 1920 to consider the feasibility of building a railway from The Pas to the ore deposit at the Flin Flon property. (Manitoba Archives)

Members of Manitoba Legislative Assembly and others, loading into canoes after a lunch break on one of the portages on the way to view the Flin Flon property. September 1920 (K. H. Williams)

Tom Creighton, in white shirt, pointing out the extent of development work to the members of the Manitoba Legislative Assembly. September 1920 (Manitoba Archives)

No. 2 shaft on the Flin Flon property being viewed by the Manitoba Legislative Assembly. September 1920 (Manitoba Archives)

The visiting group included Premier T. C. Norris and his cabinet; members of the press and several prominent business men; along with The Pas Board of Trade who had issued the invitation to visit the north.

John 'Jack' Edward Hammell, mining promoter and part owner of the Flin Flon property. (Northern Miner — 1935)

Scott Turner, consulting engineer for Mining Corporation of Canada. Turner recommended that the Mining Corporation proceed with further experimental work on the Flin Flon property. 1920-1925. (S. Turner Estate)

Robert Early Phelan, employed in 1922 by R. H. Channing Jr. as chief engineer to examine the ore body at Flin Flon. Phelan was General Manager of Hudson Bay Mining and Smelting Co., Limited 1927-1938. (P. LaPrairie)

Roscoe Henry Channing, left, in charge of the Flin Flon property and first president of Hudson Bay Mining and Smelting Co., Limited 1924-1956.
Oliver Lasby Flanagan, hydraulic engineer responsible for the construction of the Island Falls project. 1915-1943 (HBM&S)

Maurice A. Roche, left, Mine Superintendent and Assistant to the General Manager 1926-1960.
Waldron Alvord Green came to Flin Flon in 1925 as part of the group headed by R. E. Phelan. Green was Superintendent of the property 1926-1938. General Manager 1938-1957. (W. S. B. Lockhart)

Stanley Simpson carried the mail and drilling supplies between The Pas and Flin Flon. Equipment included dogs, sled and canoe. During the spring and fall the dogs hauled the canoe on the sled over the frozen lakes, while the canoe carried the dogs and sled over the open water. (Manitoba Archives 1919-1920)

Teams of horses hauled wagons across the sixteen mile portage to Lake Athapapuskow from Hayes stopping place at Sturgeon Landing. Passengers were Mrs. Tom Lamb and Mrs. Jack Hone. (J. Hone September 1926)

A barge system was used from Cranberry Portage to Flin Flon before the railway was complete. These barges carried everything to the camp site, including horses. (F. Willis 1928)

Logs were laid side by side over muskeg areas to create a 'corduroy' road. (Manitoba Archives 1925)

Dog teams were a popular sight during the northern winter months. This probably explains why dogs were so plentiful in the early days of Flin Flon (H. Ennis 1928)

An all-purpose canoe that could be pulled over the ice on runners and when open water had to be crossed the sled was removed. (H. Ennis 1928)

When nothing else was available, foot transportation on poles over the many stretches of muskeg was necessary between Wabishkok and Kisseynew Lakes on the way to Island Falls. (H. Ennis 1928)

Flin Flon camp site in the fall of 1928. Tents were set up as temporary residence for construction workers. Jack Hone's store to the right, sits in front of the site of the main shaft. (HBM&S)

Construction of pilot mill began in August 1926 and went into operation March 1927. Steam lines ran from the powerhouse on the right to the assay office and mill. (H. Ennis 1928)

A dam was built across Flin Flon Lake to allow the water to be pumped out in preparation for excavation of the ore body by open pit mining. (W. S. B. Lockhart 1928)

Flin Flon's business district situated near Flin Flon Lake consisted of Northland Drug Company, The Royal Bank of Canada and the Canadian Bank of Commerce. (F. A. Hollier 1928)

Hockey on the Flin Flon Lake rink provided many hours of recreation during the long winter months. (W. H. Barker 1928)

The many lakes along the RAILWAY ROUTE from Cranberry Portage to Flin Flon allowed access to several different points for clearing and grading ahead of the steel. (H. Guymer 1928)

Rails were laid over frozen muskeg and gravel spread to prevent thawing under the tracks during warm weather. (F. Wells 1928)

Piling for the Channing trestle was put in place during the winter months. Construction of the railway began in January 1928 and was completed by October 1928. (E. Germain 1928)

Clearing blasted rock. The side car was used for dumping gravel. (F. Wells 1928)

A rock cut along the track one mile outside of Channing (E. Germain 1928)

The Dominion Construction Company converted this car for easier transportation from one construction site to another. (F. A. Hollier 1928)

Mrs. Harry McLean holds the Golden Spike for Premier John Bracken at the completion of the line to Flin Flon in October 1928. Harry McLean, construction superintendent and Barney M. Stitt, M.P. for the Nelson Constituency look on. (H. Guymer)

Charlie B. Morgan, contractor in charge of freighting construction equipment and supplies to Island Falls during the winter of 1928-1929. (W. S. B. Lockhart)

Island Falls on the Churchill River was the site selected for the proposed power plant. January 1929 (F. Willis)

Linn tractors were equipped with snow plows and were capable of hauling up to 38 tons, the weight of this load. The huge transformer had to be transported on a specially built rack. (F. Willis 1928)

Seven of these wooden water tanks were used to ice the land stretches between the frozen lakes on the way to Island Falls. The ice covered land made travel much easier for the linn tractors and sleighs. (F. Willis 1928)

Freighting tons of equipment wasn't without mishap. The diver is preparing to hook a pulley to a sunken linn tractor on Barrier Lake. Winter 1928-1929 (Mrs. O. Volden)

September 1929, the powerhouse was compete and the transmission line approach was being installed. (F. Willis)

Flin Flon Lake drained and newly constructed company on the right. (H. Ennis 1929)

Head frame steel being erected. Mine changehouse in centre. (H. Ennis 1929)

Drilling in preparation for blasting. Bunkhouses were built to house the construction workers. (H. Ennis 1929)

Workers pouring cement. (H. Ennis 1929)

The mill steel almost completed. (H. Ennis 1929)

Erection of steel for zinc plant buildings by the Dominion Bridge Co., Limited. (H. Ennis 1929)

Custodis Chimney Company was contracted to build the two stacks. (W. S. B. Lockhart 1930)

The bunkhouses with the finishing touch — paint. The community hall and water tower on the right. (F. A. Hollier 1929)

Dinner time at the cook house. (H. Ennis 1929)

A most important day — payday at the company main office. (H. Ennis 1929)

Construction of the zinc plant — temporary powerhouse to the left. Spring 1930 (H. Ennis)

Almost ready for operation. Copper smelter and zinc plant. August 1930 (HBM&S)

Earliest method of getting water — chop a hole in the ice and fill your bucket. (H. Ennis 1928)

Flin Flon's first delivery water wagon. (Mrs. P. Dion 1929)

Working on the pipe line from Cliff Lake to the reservoir. Ole Wick, left, Vic Bowes and Les Foster. (Babe McCullum 1929)

The twenty-inch wood stave pipe line ran from Cliff Lake to the company reservoir. (H. Ennis 1929)

Building a reservoir at Flin Flon required some fill to build a dam. (HBM&S)

By 1929 some resemblance to a main street was taking shape. Charlie Young's restaurant on the right, W. S. Johnston's Boarding House on the left. Lamont's new store being constructed farther down the street. (T. Lamont 1929)

Jack Hone replaced his first log store with this modern 74' x 66' building situated just west of the company staffhouse. (F. A. Hollier 1929)

Construction of Hudson Bay Mining and Smelting required that the Northland Drug store be moved over to the townsite. (F. A. Hollier 1929)

The Royal Bank of Canada on its way to Main Street via linn tractor. (Bob Maguire 1929)

Flin Flon Draying and Transfer Company was established in 1929. Standing outside are the owners Albert Voss and Jack (Dutch) Dykhuyzen. (Mrs. G. DeVries 1929)

Pat Burns' meat market was built on the hillside facing south down Main Street. This building was later purchased by John Floch for his bakery. (Johnson & Reesor 1929)

Miss Laura Robson, Flin Flon's first teacher, taught school in the back of the United Church building on Church Street. (Bea Halliday 1929)

C.G.I.T. (Canadian Girls in Training) was organized in 1929 by Mrs. Otto Bergman — back. Left to right: Florence Gilman, Audrey Lasteen, Edlah Uhlin, Beatrice Feldmann, Jean Dow, Jean Plummer, Kathleen French, Margaret Lau, Emmy Lasteen, Marjorie Feldmann, Lorraine Freedman, Eileen Hughes and Anna Lewis. (Bea Halliday 1929)

Grades 2 to 4 were taught in the United Church. Teacher Anna Inkster. (Marg McBratney 1930)

Doris Forster, primary teacher, with her pupils outside one of the four churches used for schoolrooms during the week. (F. Wells 1930)

Classes 2, 7 and 8 in front of the Pioneer Store on Hapnot Street. Teachers — Ben Hodkinson and Miss Hazel Parker. (Bea Halliday 1931)

The first Canadian National Railway station at Flin Flon was situated at Mile 86. (J. Paylor 1930)

Jack Hone leased land near the outlet of Ross Creek on Schist Lake in April 1933 to establish Arrow Airways. Jack had been providing air service with his Avro Avian Seaplane since 1927. (J. Hone)

William Race Henderson, left, was the first postmaster for the Company and later the municipality. Henry Montagnes, radio operator, assisted 'Hendy' Henderson in the postal duties. (H. Montagnes 1928)

The first official post office on the west side of Main Street between Winnipeg Tailors and Gateways Drugs, opened August 26, 1929 with W. R. Henderson postmaster. Mail for Pelican Narrows was delivered by dog team. (H. Montagnes 1930)

18

1927 team — left to right, back row: Tom Creighton — manager, W. F. Hughes, G. G. Duncan — captain, W. K. Hutchinson, B. B. Snydal — Trainer. Sitting: D. E. Bourke, J. Hone, M. A. Clow, H. J. Hartt. Front row: Norm Stephansson and Eileen Hughes — mascots. (W. Grayson 1927)

1928 team — left to right: Dave Smith, Fred McIntosh, Doug Bourke, Cliff Setterington, Jack Moberly, Frank Guymer. Front row: Bud Murray, unidentified, Johnny Keddie. (F. A. Hollier 1928)

Ross Lake Island looking northeast. Paddy Faubert owned and operated the dance pavilion over the water. This building was later moved and rebuilt at Phantom Lake. (Flin Flon Historical Society 1930)

Part of the dance pavilion on Ross Lake. (E. VanDoorn 1931)

A closer view of the pavilion. Several diving boards were provided for all to enjoy. (E. Germain 1930)

Swimming marathon was held in 1931 with the starting point at Paddy's pavilion. (Mrs. P. Dion 1931)

For the more daring athlete log rolling was popular. (W. S. B. Lockhart 1930)

After Hudson Bay Mining and Smelting drained Flin Flon Lake, the dried flat lake bottom became an excellent sports ground. It was the only lake bottom golf course in the world. George Sanford and Clarence Merrell tee off. (G. Sanford 1936)

Basketball in Flin Flon was played outdoors. (E. W. Gohl 1930)

Pole vaulting was part of the sports day activities on the lake bottom July 1, 1930. (L. Lapointe)

Sports at Hapnot Lake July 1, 1929. (G. Sanford)

Tug-Of-War was a favourite with many at the July 1, 1930 sports day (H. Ennis)

21

Flin Flon Community Hall was erected in 1929 to provide the growing settlement with facilities, equipment and meeting place. (HBM&S)

The Music Miners of 1929: In doorway: Paul Sharpe, Ralph Bloomfield. Front row, left to right: Charlie Spence, Wes Sevailes, Don McLean, Monty Holmes, Frank Thompson and Steinie Thorsteinsson. This group was the original 'music makers' in Flin Flon and played for dances held at the staffhouse. (W. S. B. Lockhart)

The Happy Ramblers — a band sponsored by the B.P.O. Elks Lodge which was instituted in April 1930. This band was under the direction of Charlie Bosshardt. The original members were: George Chaiiko, Mike Magnusson, Erick Malila, Ingvald Hanson, Carl Sandstrom, Bert Wielenga, Herman Cavanaugh and Pete Storjord. (Marg McBratney 1931)

Babe McCormick, company stenographer, was Queen of The Pas Dog Derby in 1929. (W. S. B. Lockhart)

Flin Flon Branch 73 of the Canadian Legion B.E.S.L. was established in October 1929. Dr. Ernest J. Kelly was elected first president. (Tom Mann)

September 1, 1931 — LEADING CANADIANS PAY VISIT TO LOCAL PLANT ON CHAMBER COMMERCE TRIP. A hearty welcome was extended to over two hundred and fifty members of the Chamber of Commerce on their way to Churchill on their pre-convention tour. The party consisted of three provincial premiers from Nova Scotia, Saskatchewan and Manitoba, senators and cabinet ministers and leading men of organizations all over the entire Dominion. (Credit) Manitoba Archives

West side of Main Sreet — September 1, 1931. (Credit) Manitoba Archives

East side of Main Street — September 1, 1931. (Credit) Manitoba Archives

West side of Main Street 1929. Left to right: D. J. Lowry's Barber Shop; J. Dremain, owner of Winnipeg Tailors and Furriers; W. R. Henderson's building (later Post Office); and Gateway Drugs. (Bill Kirkwood)

Having a problem unloading beer kegs for delivery to Corona Hotel — 1931. (Bea Halliday)

Main Street looking north — 1930. Left to right: Flin Flon Realty owned and operated by L. Moore and B. Stitt; Flin Flon Fruit and Produce; Keddie's Hardware; Blue Goose Confectionary; F. A. Schieder and Royal Bank. (Ed VanDoorn)

By the fall of 1931 drainage ditches had been installed along Main Street alleviating the water problem. (S. Strindland)

W. F. Hughes (left) sold his business to A. Ostry in 1931. (Art Dodds 1929)

Bell's Hardware was adjacent to Hughes. (Art Dodds 1929)

North end of Ross Lake Island 1929. (Milt Laing)

Foot bridge across to west side of Ross Lake Island. (Jack Johnson 1930)

Foot bridge from east side of Ross Lake Island to mainland. (W. S. B. Lockhart 1930)

"Sippel's Hill" (Ross Street) named after Dell Sippel who used this route to deliver groceries to the Ross Lake area. (HBM&S 1930)

Hudson Bay Mining and Smelting Co., Limited before the excavation of the OPEN PIT. (HBM&S 1931)

One of the largest blasts in the open pit was 150 tons of dynamite in 1931. Residents were warned prior to blast time and urged to remain in their homes. One story is told of rocks flying through a window and into a pot of potatoes. (Bea Halliday)

After blasting, railway tracks were laid for the electric locomotives. The old office perches on the edge of the pit. (H. Ennis 1931)

Electric Marian shovels loaded the loose rock into the 22 yard side dump cars for delivery to the crusher. (Flin Flon Historical Society 1931)

The old pilot mill still stands in 1983 on the edge of the open pit. (H. Ennis 1931)

South end of open pit. The railway tracks were moved many times during the years of open pit mining. No. 2 shaft and shafthouse at top centre. (E. W. Gohl 1931)

Main School officially opened Thursday, September 1, 1932, with ten rooms available to accommodate four hundred pupils. (Art Dodds)

Teacher Audrey (Hall) Merrell and her class outside the newly constructed Main School. (Mrs. P. Krassilowsky 1932)

Main School, modern and up to date. Doris (Forster) Holmes and her elementary class. (Mrs. P. Krassilowsky 1932)

Another class of Main School students — teacher not known. (Mrs. P. Krassilowsky 1932)

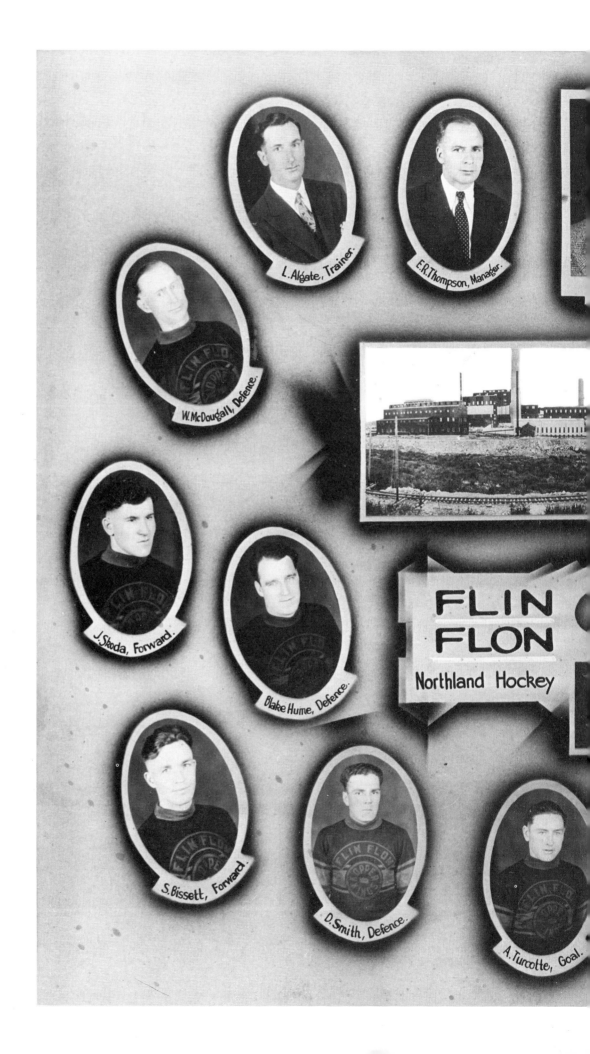

L. Algate, Trainer.

E. R. Thompson, Manager.

W. McDougall, Defence.

J. Skoda, Forward.

Blake Hume, Defence.

FLIN FLON

Northland Hockey

S. Bissett, Forward.

D. Smith, Defence.

A. Turcotte, Goal.

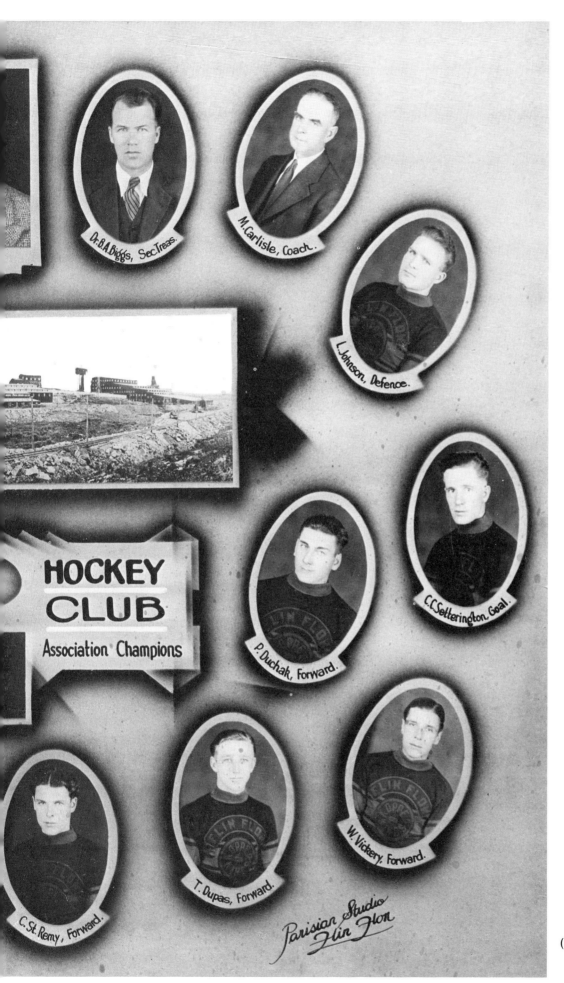

HOCKEY CLUB
Association Champions

Dr. B.A. Biggs, Sec. Treas.

M. Carlisle, Coach.

L. Johnson, Defence.

P. Duchak, Forward.

C.C. Setterington, Goal.

C. St. Remy, Forward.

T. Dupas, Forward.

W. Vickery, Forward.

Parisian Studio
Flin Flon

Phantom Lake in 1932 provided summer recreation for the people of Flin Flon. Paddy Faubert's dance hall under construction far right. (K. Allen)

Phantom Lake had activities for everyone — camping, bingo games, dancing and swimming. (J. Maitland 1933)

A summer day at Phantom Lake. (J. Paylor 1934)

MAYOR, MEMBERS & OFFICIALS
FIRST COUNCIL OF THE
MUNICIPAL DISTRICT of FLIN FLON
1933-34

(Flin Flon Historical Society).

Mushers lined up for the start of the 1933 race. Alphonse Chartrand from The Pas was the trophy winner. (F. Wells)

The Hendy Trophy was donated by W. R. 'Hendy' Henderson in 1931 to the winner of the JUNIOR DOG MUSHING CHAMPIONSHIP RACE. This race was a 9½ mile run from the Flin Flon Hotel to Mandy Mine and return. Races were run weekly with the winners racing against each other in the final run for the trophy. W. R. Henderson died on November 28, 1938 and the Elks Lodge took over the sponsorship of the races until 1941, when the expense of keeping dogs during the war years became too much of a burden. (H. Montagnes)

Junior Dog Racing was a well attended sport. Fergus Streamer of Cranberry Portage won the race in February 1934 and again in 1935. (A. Plummer)

Warren Plummer, shown with W. R. Henderson, was the first winner of the Hendy Trophy with a time of 1 hour, 12 minutes and 14 seconds on March 7, 1931. (A. Plummer)

February 18, 1936 was a tough year on dogs and sleds because of the 'Bonspiel Thaw'. Billy Kelly won both the 1936 and 1937 races. (E. Germain)

Other trophy winners were 1932 — Florence May, 1938 — Gordon Kelly, 1939 and 1940 — Fred Slade of Cranberry Portage.

William Race Henderson, one of the founders of Reg'lar Fellers (1933), an organization for boys of all ages that emphasized camping and sportsmanship. (Kay Fagrie)

The first camping trip taken by the Reg'lar Fellers to Marie Lake, Hendy Henderson on left, Buck Hay on right. (T. Mann 1933)

A Bean Feed was held at the Community Hall with Joe Stone cooking the feast. George Warey, one of the leaders on extreme left. (T. Mann 1935)

The Reg'lar Fellers participated in the Silver Jubilee Parade May 6, 1935. (Babe McCullum)

Reg'lar Fellers at their annual camp held in 1935 at Island Falls. (H. Montagnes)

Reg'lar Fellers leaving for Athawaku Beach at Athapap Siding. Premier John Bracken and Hendy Henderson with the boys. (T. Mann 1936)

The month-long strike (June 9 to July 9, 1934) forced the closure of the Company. (J. Paylor)

Approximately 92 members of the Royal Canadian Mounted Police were stationed in Flin Flon during the final week of the dispute. (W. B. S. Lockhart)

Voters at the Community Hall were met with opposition on Saturday, June 30, 1934. (F. A. Hollier)

Leaders of the strike were arrested and escorted to the station by RCMP. (Manitoba Archives July 6, 1934)

On July 9, 1934 the men marched back to work. (W. B. S. Lockhart)

Hapnot School officially opened on November 26, 1934. (Ken Allen)

Ross Lake School was built in 1935. (J. Paylor)

George B. Mainwaring — Mayor of Flin Flon 1935 and 1936. (J. Paylor)

The Post Office (right) moved off Main Street to First Avenue in 1931 and was remodelled in June 1933. The CNR Station opened officially in December 1934. (M. Laing)

The second storey of the Post Office was enlarged in November 1935. (Bal Biggs)

On May 6, 1935, Flin Flon paid tribute to King George and Queen Mary on their Silver Jubliee. The Canadian Legion supervised the preparation for the parade under Marshal J. D. McMartin, President of the Legion. (W. B. S. Lockhart)

The most spectacular float of the parade was constructed by the B.P.O. Elks, titled "On Guard". A mamoth aluminum elk stood over a miniature of the Elks Home. (W. B. S. Lockhart)

The Canadian Slovak League attired in blue shirts, followed their float. They were awarded a special prize for the best organized unit. (W. B. S. Lockhart)

The Hungarian Cultural Society Dancers, some of which were Louis Tusz, Paul Huszti, Mrs. J. Halasz, Emily and Marta Balogh. (W. B. S. Lockhart)

The Hollanders' float won first prize. Those on the float were Albert Voss, Nuiskes Bros., Jim Aplin, Lena Van-Doorn, Tom Heyland, Mr. and Mrs. Len VanderWal. (W. B. S. Lockhart)

The Danes, dressed in ancient garb of the Vikings, took second prize. (L. Johnson)

The Medical Services provided the Royal Coach drawn by four horses. Seated inside were Emile Arsenault and Svea Sjoberg, winners of the King and Queen Contest. Other contestants acted as King's pages. (W. B. S. Lockhart)

St. James Church building was started in 1931, and officially opened by Bishop Thomas on July 7, 1931. (St. James Church)

Rev. R. F. Dawson came to Flin Flon May 3, 1931 to preach at St. James Anglican Church. (St. James Church)

St. Augustine's Church, right and the Salvation Army Hall, left, situated on Church Street. (J. Paylor September 1934)

St. Augustine's Church being moved across Church Street to the lot formerly occupied by G. B. Mainwaring's residence. Mainwaring's house was moved to the former church site beside the Salvation Army Hall. St. Augustine was dedicated to St. Ann in October 1935. (J. Paylor September 1934)

First Pentecostal Church was built in 1935. (Pentecostal Church)

First preacher of the Pentecostal Church, Rev. Martin McCullum married Mary Mandziuk in 1935. (Pentecostal Church)

The Legion Hall was first constructed at 73 Church Street in 1936. This photograph was taken during World War II as event by the huge 'V for Victory' sign on the face of the building. (Flin Flon Historical Society)

The Legion sponsored a Drum and Bugle Band. (T. Mann 1936)

The Elks Home officially opened November 14, 1933. The huge aluminum elk outside the building was part of the Elks' float in May 1935. (Milt Laing)

The Rotary Club held a fund raising drive to purchase a fire truck which was presented to the Town on October 31, 1936. (Jack Sturley)

North end of Main Street — sidewalks were completed and the roadway built up with gravel. (Babe McCullum 1936)

Construction of the Corona Hotel began in late 1929 and was later destroyed by fire on December 6, 1955. The brick fire walls are evident beside the Corona and Royal Hotel farther down the street. (Reminder October 1937)

The stairs led from Hill Street down to Third Avenue. (J. Paylor 1935)

Third Avenue hill. (Bea Halliday 1935)

Pilings for the bridge to Ross Lake Island were installed in September 1936. (Chuck Donald)

Appeals for contributions were made in the fall of 1934 with construction started early in 1935. Sheathing on the curling rink near completion. (Flin Flon Historical Society)

Steel for the ice arena being erected. (Flin Flon Historical Society 1935)

Community Club Ice Arena and Curling Rink. General Hospital at top left. (W. B. S. Lockhart 1939)

Jubilee Park Rink opened on December 18, 1937, at the corner of Bellevue and Third Avenues. The park was named in honor of the celebration of the Silver Jubilee of King George V. (Flin Flon Historical Society)

Jubilee Park Rink was used by all ages — looking north up Callinan Lane. (Watson Gilmore 1943)

(Watson Gilmore)

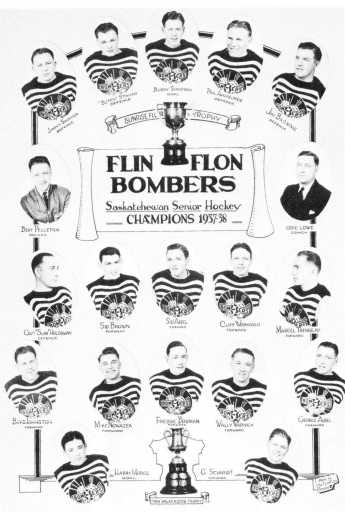

(Laurie Johnson)

Welcome Home Bombers, winners of the Saskatchewan Senior Hockey League.
(Sid Brown April 1938)

George W. Evans, Mayor of Flin Flon 1937 and
1938. (Flin Flon Historical Society)

45

The steel arch at the intersection of Main Street and First Avenue was decorated with evergreens, streamers and flags in honor of the Coronation of King George VI on May 12, 1937. (W. B. S. Lockhart)

The first prize winning float was the French Canadian depicting Cartier's discovery of Canada. (W. B. S. Lockhart)

Second prize was awarded to the Polish White Eagle Society. (W. B. S. Lockhart)

A basket of 'American Beauties' gained third place honors. This float was entered by the citizens of the United States. (W. B. S. Lockhart)

The Chinese entry had a huge lion head on the radiator of the truck and on the cab perched a gay Pagoda. (W. B. S. Lockhart)

The Knights of Columbus float showed a Knight with his sword protecting the flag and cross from the huge green dragon. (W. B. S. Lockhart)

The Icelandic float represented a mountain over which the 'Maid of the Mountain' held sway. (W. B. S. Lockhart)

H.B.M.& S's entry exemplified the Irish Free State with a huge harp of gold. 'Irishmen' distributed clay pipes to the spectators. It was rumored that George Mainwaring had the harp decorating his lawn the day after the parade. (W. B. S. Lockhart)

Australia was entered by the B.P.O. Elks. The gigantic kangaroo and Maori warrier rode in state. (W. B. S. Lockhart)

The Independent Order of Odd Fellows' float displayed the Canadian Coats of Arms. (W. B. S. Lockhart)

The Jugo-Slav Canadian Association float was adorned with a large crown while musicians in native costume played their folk music. (W. B. S. Lockhart)

'Tulip Time', the Dutch entry was complete with a cottage, windmill and three thousand tulips embedded in the imitation garden. (W. B. S. Lockhart)

The B.P.O. Elks Grand Lodge Convention was held in Flin Flon in July 1937. (Flin Flon Historical Society)

Grand Lodge Convention, B.P.O.E., Flin Flon, Man., 1952

July 1, 1936 celebrations at the corner of Main Street and Third Avenue was well attended. (Vic Bowes)

Drilling competitions were an annual event during the July 1st celebrations held at Phantom Lake. (Mrs. DeVries 1937)

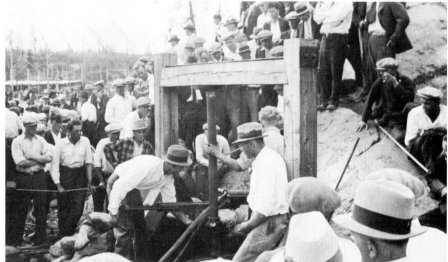

Flin Flon Club 27 celebrate their tenth anniversary at the Legion Hall December 1, 1937. (Flin Flon Historical Society)

Flin Flon General Hospital was opened officially on December 10, 1938. St. Ann's Church to the left. (W. B. S. Lockhart)

Dr. Harry Marantz, owner of the Cottage Clinic on Hapnot Street. The Clinic closed its doors in November 1938 when the General Hospital opened. (A. Plummer)

The Robertson Hospital had to relocated from the road allowance on Third Avenue and Main Street to Main and Fourth. It remained in use as a hospital until 1938. (Lorna F. Young)

Although Dr. P. C. Robertson was the owner of his hospital he did not arrive in Flin Flon to take charge until January 14, 1938. (Lorna F. Young)

Dr. Percy Johnson, Dr. Harvey McNichol and Nurse Ruby McSorley. (D. Jobin 1940)

Dr. Norman Stephansson and Dr. Glen Willson at Phantom Lake. (HBM&S 1940's)

Company Hospital 1944. (HBM&S)

(Art Wahlenberg)

FLIN FLON SCOTTISH "BURNS" ANNIVERSARY BANQUET. JANUARY 25, 1938. FLIN FLON MANITOBA.

Bill McKeen hauling water for delivery. (Bill Leask 1939)

Harold Leask started his draying service in Flin Flon in 1934. He moved from the Halfway on the Phantom Lake Road to the Barn Area in 1937. (B. Leask)

Leask bought the garage owned by Ford Dealer Reg Cardell in 1937. The name changed to Reliance Services in 1940. (Bill Leask)

From horse and dray to trucks. (D. Baird 1941)

Bus Service was operated by T. H. Doxey with a fleet of five buses. Doxey and Bill Axtell beside the Lake View Bus September 1, 1938. (B. Axtell)

The bus depot was at the north west end of Main Street in 1938. (B. Axtell)

54

Keddie Trophy winner 1938 Bonspiel. Standing: Tex Douglas, Sam Hankin. Seated Al Ball, F. F. Bennett (skip). (Flin Flon Historical Society)

Flin Flon Fire Department was the winner of the Fire Drill Contest held on July 1st, 1938. Left to right: A. A. Sparrow, V. Lundt, J. Wurtach, G. Ekstrom, H. Lundstrom, E. Hoglander, Otto Klutz Fire Chief, and mascot Bing, the Boston Bulldog. (City of Flin Flon)

Flag raising on May 24, 1939, with the Elks Band and Legion Drum and Bugle 'Boys' providing the music. (Mrs. D. Low)

All eyes are on the Canadian Flag as it is raised on May 24, 1939. (Mrs. D. Low)

Main School Playground was the setting for the May 24, 1939 celebration. (Mrs. D. Low)

Civic Decoration Day Parade going passed Jubilee Playground on the way to the Ross Lake Cemetery August 6, 1939. (H. Hobbs)

More of the Decoration Day Parade. (Mrs. A. Hudak)

Joe Pallanik, owner of Joe's Taxi Service, had the honor of chauffeuring His Excellency during his stay in Flin Flon. (Flin Flon Historical Society)

Mayor Peter McSheffrey welcomes Lord Tweedsmuir, Governor General of Canada, to Flin Flon on August 9, 1939. (Flin Flon Historical Society)

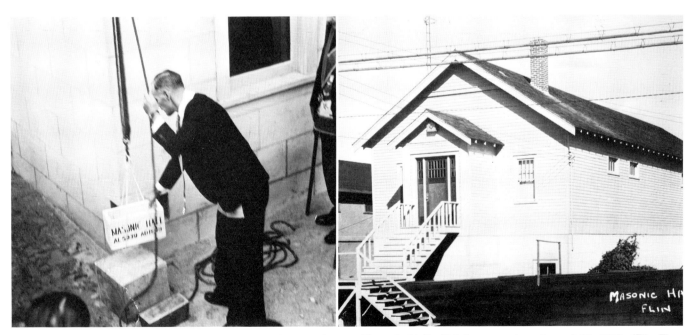

Flin Flon Masonic Lodge celebrated their tenth anniversary by laying of the corner stone on August 12, 1939. (Flin Flon Masonic Lodge)

Masonic Hall officially opened on August 12, 1939. (Flin Flon Masonic Lodge)

Women were enthusiastic ball players. The 'Cubs' and Senior Ball Teams of 1939. (Dodie Stewart)

Foster Park Tennis Court opened on August 25, 1939. Looking west with Ross Lake School Playground in foreground. (D. Baird)

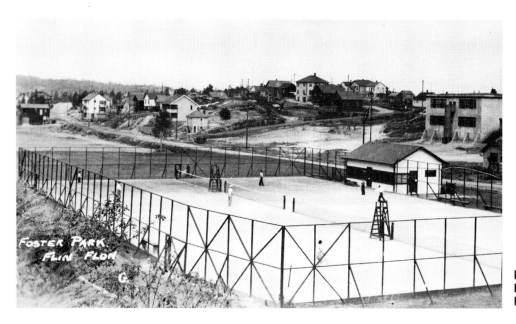

Looking northeast — Ross Lake School on the right. (Flin Flon Historical Society)

58

Jubilee Playground was a popular ball diamond in the summer and home of the Zinc Moguls Softball Team. (D. Baird 1940)

Manitoba Intermediate Basketball Champions 1939 and 1940. Back row, left to right: Jack Honeyman, Art Peebles, Jimmy Goodman, Jimmy Hewitt. Front row: Edgar Henry, Hector McCaig, Barney Marantz, Eric Barker. Sitting: Ernie Butterworth. (Flin Flon Historical Society)

FLIN FLON COLLEGIATE INSTITUTE
GRADUATING CLASS 1942

MICHAEL SIRU   LORETTA KERSCHSTEIN   COLIN MANN   ISABELLE HOLMES   RAYMOND ANDERSON   ELSIE EDWARDS

HENRY DRINNAN   JOHN WILSON B.A.   IVAN HAMILTON B.A. MED.   K.M. HEYES B.A.   ROBERT ROCHE

NORMA WALDRON   BETTY CALLIN   VIRGINIA IANNONE   JOYCE SWICK   JOYCE JOHNSON   JUNE PENNOCK   DOROTHY YOUNG

WALTER BRODEY   ROBERT BURKETT   JOHN GREENAWAY   AUBREY NORQUAY   DONALD McRAE   WELLESLEY WEESE

PATRICIA KITCHEN   BERNICE JOHNSON   ENID GRAY   VIOLET GOODMANSON   MARITA COYNE   FRANCES BRUHNSEN

(HBM&S)

Hapnot Collegiate 1942. (HBM&S)

Teaching Staff 1942-1943. (HBM&S)

North end of Ross Lake Island — Curling Rink (top left) was officially opened November 27, 1941. (Circle C St. James Church)

Looking east across Ross Lake subdivision — school to the right. (W. B. S. Lockhart 1938 to 1941)

Sippel Hill in the early 1940's. (Bea Halliday)

Looking northwest from bottom of Sippel Hill. Ski Jump at top right. (Hec McCaig early 1940's)

CFAR officially opened on November 14, 1937, broadcasting on a three hour a day schedule from 120 Main Street. (G. H. Grindle)

J. M. 'Monty' Bridgman, owner of Monty's Radio and Auto Shop (see left), applied for a licence under Arctic Radio Corporation in May 1937. (W. B. S. Lockhart)

CFAR relocated from Main Street to 75 Callinan in September 1941, under new ownership. (Ted Wright)

CFAR studios remained at 75 Callinan for thirty years. (Doug O'Brien)

Dr. B. A. Biggs, head of Rotary Club, appealed for funds over CFAR for the purchase of an iron lung. (Rotary Club October 1938)

A Victory Loan Campaign was planned by the following committee who held a meeting in the Golden Gate Cafe on February 22, 1942: Left to right: Bruce Weese, PR Director; Mayor Orson F. Wright (who had just been named King's Council); Premier John Bracken; Harry J. Miles, Editor of Flin Flon Miner; George Murton; Tom McMurray, Winnipeg Divisional Oganizer; L. F. 'Concrete' McDonald, General Chairman; George Salverson, CFAR; John Ambrose, Vice Chairman; Fred Willis, Deputy Mayor; A. W. Klieforth, US Consul General; Frank Blackburn; standing are Lloyd Fairbairn and D. B. Shaw. (Flin Flon Archives)

Hudson Bay Mining and Smelting Co., Limited Pipe Band was formed in 1942. Left to right: W. Burnett, F. Stewart, Rick Fraser, Pinkie Davie, Bill Duncan, Slim Holdaway, Ed Hammill, W. Davie, R. McKenzie and Bert Kirkwood. (Mrs. Eva Johnson)

Decoration Day Parade headed by Mayor Orson Wright, Rev. R. Horsefield and the Pipe Band — August 1, 1943. (HBM&S)

Women worked in the Zinc Plant during World War II — 1943. (HBM&S)

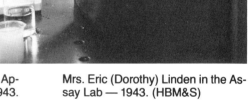

And in the Rubber Application Plant — 1943. (HBM&S)

Mrs. Eric (Dorothy) Linden in the Assay Lab — 1943. (HBM&S)

The girls in the Machine Shop — 1943. (HBM&S)

Mrs. Ann Kulcher loading zinc in the Casting Plant — 1943. (HBM&S)

Phantom Lake Tennis Courts — 1942. (HBM&S)

Bandstand at Phantom Lake with the Elks Band performing — July 1, 1941. (Hazel Evans)

Old dock at Phantom Lake — 1942. (HBM&S)

Cement stairs on the west side of Phantom Lake — July 1, 1944. (HBM&S)

Hudson Bay Mining and Smelting took over the operation and upkeep of Phantom Lake in 1943, replacing the old dock with a wider one. (HBM&S)

Second dock was accessible only by water in 1943. (HBM&S)

The Community Hall served as a Kindergarten in the 1940's. (HBM&S)

Mrs. McPherson's Kindergarten Class of 1943 was the winner of the Percussion Band Shield in the Music Festival. (Bill Kirkwood)

Mrs. Ruth McPherson's Kindergarten Class of 1942. (Bill Kirkwood)

Grade IV and V at Ross Lake School — October 1944. (Mrs. D. Baird)

Mrs. McPherson and Mrs. F. Rogers with the class of 1945 at the Community Hall. (Slim Holdaway)

Northminster United Church Choir, winners of the Rotary Trophy for adult vocal group — 1944. Front row (left to right) — Mrs. W. Cole, Margaret McLean, Mrs. A. Rogers, Mrs. P. Nowosad, Mrs. J. A. Bell (Director), Mrs. E. Butterworth, Pearl Leask, Mrs. W. Burrows, Helen Smith. Second row — Eileen Hanley, Mrs. S. Rumbal, Jean Morrice, Yvonne Cross, Anna Lewis, Mrs. P. Young, Dorothy Young, Joyce Johnson, Mrs. C. Spice. Back row — Gordon Gadd, Ernie Bucher, C. Lewthwaite, Harold Vance, W. Lewthwaite, Thomas Patching and Seth Matthews. (Kit Cole)

Mrs. Bell's Junior Musical Club, winners of the Hudson's Bay Company Shield for junior vocal ensemble. Front row (left to right) Joan Gebhardt, Joanne Miles, Nadia Nowosad, Marilyn Burrows, Helen Rogers, Ruth McIsaac, Donna Aspevig, Avonne Horkoff, Mary Sabo. Second row — June Pennock, Frances Bruhnson, Areta Evans, Janet Roche, Margaret Nasselquist, Theresa Iannone, Dorothy Hogoboam, Eleanor Pennock, Virginia Iannone. Back row — Margaret Tothe, Joan Ash, Elizabeth Roche, Joyce Johnson, Violet Goodmanson, Mrs. J. A. Bell (Director), Katherine Wrye, June Lamont, Margaret McLean and Lana Chin. (Marg McBratney 1944)

The Flin Flon Medical Services opened their Clinic on Church Street in 1944. (W. B. S. Lockhart)

Municipal Hall with Honor Roll — 1941. (Flin Flon Archives)

Cyril Steventon was Mayor from 1944 to 1952. (Flin Flon Historical Society)

The Honor Roll listing the names of 1380 men and women from Flin Flon who joined the armed services in World War II was dedicated on September 16, 1941. (W. B. S. Lockhart)

Returning veterans of World War II — Welcome Home Celebrations were held August 5, 1946. (J. Paylor)

Welcome Home Parade ended up at Phantom Lake where 12,000 buns and 11,000 weiners were handed out free to the veterans and their families — August 5, 1946. (HBM&S)

3200 free ice cream cones were also handed out to the children of the veterans — August 5, 1946. (HBM&S)

Dominion Day (July 1, 1946) at Phantom Lake included races for the kids — (HBM&S)

As well as rides on the merry-go-round. (HBM&S)

Willowvale was the site of new homes built by the Company and purchased by returning veterans — 1946. (HBM&S)

Northminster United Church being built — 1946. (HBM&S)

One storey at the front, three at the back. (Reminder)

Not quite complete. (HBM&S)

Hill Street had to be raised to meet the front entrance. (Reminder)

Completed. (W. B. S. Lockhart)

The Flin Flon Kinsmen Club was chartered on April 7, 1946 and held their first Halloween Costume Party that year. (Lorna F. Young)

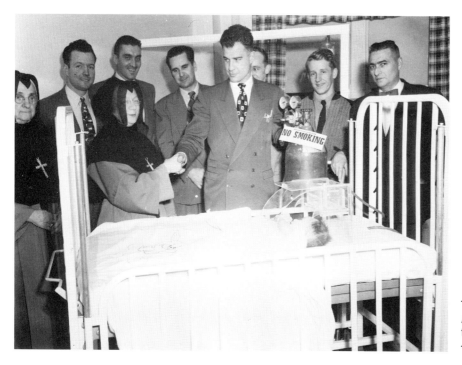

The Flin Flon Rotary Club supplied an Armstrong Portable Incubator to be used in the Delivery Room of the General Hospital — March 7, 1946. (T. Dobson)

Girl Guides, Dorothy Low, Captain, 1938. (Hazel Evans)

Flin Flon's first group of Girl Guides 1935. (Mrs. A. Folkestone)

Girl Guides, Ruth Shomperlen, Captain. (R. Shomperlen)

Brownies at Phantom Lake, Ruth Shomperlen, Brown Owl. (Lorna Young)

Mayor Cyril Steventon leading the settlers on their way to lease lots in Creighton, July 16, 1947. (L. W. Lee)

Gerry Quinney, CFAR Manager and A. I. Bereskin watch as Tom Creighton drives token stake to officially open the townsite of Creighton, July 16, 1947. (L. W. Lee)

Willowvale School held its first classes in November 1948. (HBM&S)

Hapnot School about 1949. (Reminder)

Birchview School was added onto in 1950. (Reminder)

Some of Flin Flon's teachers. (H. Hobbs)

Grade 4 of Terrace School won seven awards at the Music Festival, D. Ash, conductor. (D. K. Ash)

Reception for Donna Grescoe, violinist, was sponsored by the Business and Professional Women's Club, October 1949. Left to right — Ruby Arndt, Molly Wright, Bette McKenna, Donna Grescoe, Norma Tissot, Eva Wedienhammer, Dorothy Ash and Laura Glazer. (D. K. Ash)

Legion Ladies' Auxiliary, 1946. (B. Hughes)

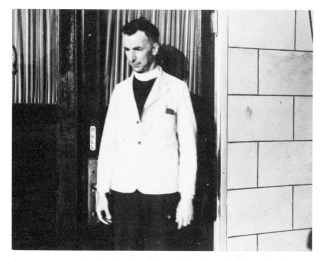

Canon Ray Horsefield, Legion Padre, 1948. (HBM&S)

Canadian Legion on parade for Decoration Day 1948. (HBM&S)

Chamber of Commerce on their annual outing to Island Falls, September 1948. (Bill Leask)

Flin Flon Lodge #57 of the Independent Order of Oddfellows, 1949. (HBM&S)

Jubilee Hall contained dance hall and public library in the early 1950's. (Ted Wright)

Mayor Cyril Steventon and Howard McIntosh outside the Fire Hall, summer 1948. (HBM&S)

St. James Anglican Church was completed in May 1948. (HBM&S)

Canon R. B. Horsefield broadcasting in Cree over CFAR, 1948. (R. B. Horsefield)

Lutheran Church, Hill Street, 1948. (HBM&S)

Salvation Army, Church Street, 1948. (HBM&S)

Governor General Viscount Alexander of Tunis visited Flin Flon on September 16 and 17, 1948. Bill Vatcher and Harry Miles look on. Mayor Steventon escorted His Excellency. (Flin Flon Archives)

Governor General inspects local units at Foster Park. (Flin Flon Archives)

Legionettes, winner of the Junior Basketball Crown of Manitoba, 1948. Back row — left to right — Signe Jacobson, Erla Dahlgren, Joan Barr, Velda Chisholm, Gwen Jackson, Joanne Miles and Jean Hoey. Front row — Enid Ransom, Avonne Horkoff, Jim Mills (Ass't Coach), Joan Setterington, Hec McCaig (Coach), Lois Miles and Doris Betteridge. (Hec McCaig)

Legionettes welcomed home. (Reminder)

Girls' hockey team, 1949. (J. Henderson)

Glee Club's first production 'Pirates of Penzance', 1947, grand finale with complete cast. (Kit Cole)

'Down in the Valley', 1949, with Carlisle Mayes and Jean Plaxton. (J. E. Goodman)

'Pinafore', March 1950. (Ellen Grose)

Elks' Christmas Cheer Broadcast, 1949. (HBM&S)

Flin Flon Junior Band outside Northland Theatre, 1949. (HBM&S)

Vickery's 'Festival Funsters', organized by Roy Vickery to play at the Trappers' Festival, February 1954. (Reminder)

Rhythm Kings, Wes Vickery, manager at piano, 1950. (Reminder)

Proud winners at Labour Day Sports. (HBM&S)

Rotary Horticultural Exhibition 1948. Left to right — Tina Konik (Queen), Lorraine Bulow and Eileen Kepper. (Reminder)

Kids Cordwood Bonspiel, Willowvale outdoor rink, 1949. (HBM&S)

Hugh Doran's rink took top honors in the Cordwood Bonspiel. (HBM&S)

The Grayling Club used 'Velvet Acres' Miniature Golf Course proceeds to purchase Peterborough canoes, summer 1949. (Reminder)

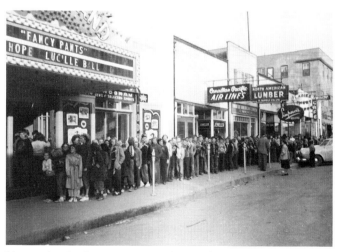

Line up for the first show, 1949. (HBM&S)

BPO Elks Annual Kingo with the Grand Prize being an automobile. Left to Right: John Kepper, Pete Lungal, Lodge Secretary Doris Ebensen, Mr. Lavergne winner of the car, Irene Leafloor, Jim Atkinson Exalted Ruler, and Joe Duffner (late 50's). (Reminder)

Bowling trophy for ten pins at the Elks Lanes donated by Kipp Kelly, 1949. (HBM&S)

Order of the Royal Purple celebrate 21st anniversary, spring 1952. (E. Cutt)

Elks' Lodge sponsored Youth Band, Jule Hampson in front, 1950. (HBM&S)

Chamber of Commerce Motorcade to The Pas to boost our highway, February 1949. (HBM&S)

Christmas tree at the intersection of Main and Third, 1949. (HBM&S)

Hicken's Shoe Service, late 1940's. (Reminder)

Milt Young, owner of Milt's Place on Main Street — 'The Sweet Shop of the North'. (Ken Allen)

Bud Jobin was elected to The Pas constituency, October 1949. (Reminder)

Daily Reminder on North Avenue, 1949. (Reminder)

North of 53 Consumers COOP Limited opened in 1949. (Cal Berry)

The COOP Garage came later. (Reminder)

COOP Coffee Bar was on the main floor, 1950. (Reminder)

The Royal Drugs Lunch Counter, 1954. (Reminder)

Mr. and Mrs. Maurice Knechtel married one hour, Mr. and Mrs. Sam Young married fifty years. (Reminder)

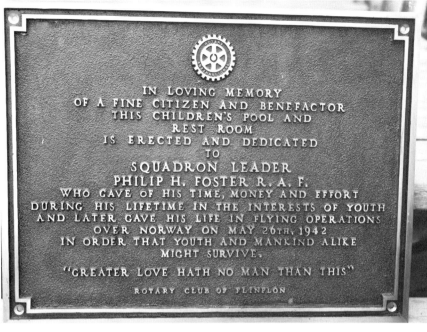

Plaque unveiled July 28, 1950. (Reminder)

Philip H. Foster. (J. Paylor)

Dedication Services of Paddling Pool and Memorial Plaque in honour of the late Sqdn. Leader Philip H. Foster, Rotary Children's Park, July 28, 1950. (Reminder)

Plaque unveiled by A. M. Walker, President of the Rotary Club. (Reminder)

The Diaper Derby was an annual event held at Rotary Park. (Reminder)

Rotary Park. (W. B. S. Lockhart)

Howard Doxey, owner of Northern Bus Lines, shakes hands with John Koval. Manager — Steve Andrusiak and wife Nettie look on, June 1950. (S. Andrusiak)

Ambulance keys handed to Mayor C. Steventon by Fire Chief Walter Redman at close of the Elks' annual carnival, June 27, 1950. Back row, left to right — Walter Redman, Don Still, Charlie Jones, Fred Berry, Vern Keats, Walter Jones. Front row — Bert Thompson, Charlie Dickens, Don McKee, Harry Brydon and Tommy Leel. (Flin Flon Historical Society)

Lieut. Gov. the Hon. R. F. McWilliams cuts copper ribbon held by F. Wildgoose of Can. Liquid Air and Mayor C. Steventon, to officially open No. 10 Highway, Bakers' Narrows, July 11, 1951. (Reminder)

Bridge Club — left to right, Mmes. Allan, Magnusson, Lewis, Dow, Hutchinson, Hopkins, McIntosh, Mardis, Thomson and Bowes, 1950. (Babe McCullum)

Rotary Club 1949. (HBM&S)

Canadian Legion Broadcasting Committee. Back row, left to right, Jim Wardle, Jim Emery, Buck Witney. Front row, Tommy Nelson, Jack Balfour, Bill Lockhart and Clare Sparling. (Flin Flon Historical Society 1951)

Club 27 lady members, December 1951. Left to right, Mmes. Lamb, Hone, Green and Akert. (Club 27)

1950-1951 Flin Flon Bombers. Left to Right: Ev. Clarkson, Herb Schiller, Len Hilton, Bob Sequin, Bob Hosegood, Hugh McKay, Eddy Taylor, Ken Peterson, Hec McCaig, Bill Tyshko, Bud Simpson, Art Harris, Harry Harasyn, Don Busch, Nick Pyevach, Stew. Reid, Marv Hunt, Bob Arneil, Alex Shibicky. (Hec McCaig)

Mayor C. Steventon and Councillor Alex Imrie watch as Too-Too opens local bonspiel, 1951. (HBM&S)

Mayor Cyril Steventon and his Council, 1951. Left to right, Bob Frederickson, Fred Willis, Earl McDonald, George Murton, Cyril Steventon, Forest Green, Bill Calvert and Alex Imrie. (HBM&S)

Northern Drama Festival Winner 'Rise and Shine'. Cast, Jim Digby, Joyce Walker, Marilyn Keddie and Stevie Stevenson, 1951. (D. K. Ash)

Youth Week Parade, May 5, 1951. (Reminder)

Mayor Steventon reads proclamation, with Ray Adams, Youth Chairman of Health and Safety Committee and Canon R. B. Horsefield looking on. May 5, 1951. (HBM&S)

Mayor Steventon hands over the reigns of office of Mayor to Metro Dmitriw, May 5, 1951. (HBM&S)

Christmas Party for children of Greek Orthodox Church, December 1951. (HBM&S)

Mrs. B. Keddie and her son Andrew, mail $1025.61 to 'Bread for Greece', proceeds from the local campaign, December 1, 1951. (Reminder)

92

Parking meters, August 7, 1950. (Reminder)

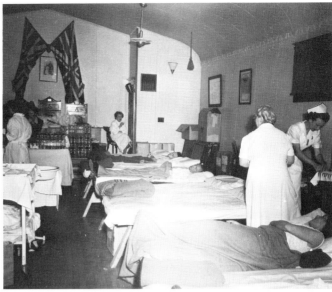

Blood Donor Clinic at the Masonic Hall, 1951. (HBM&S)

Post Office, June 11, 1951. (Reminder)

Official opening of Federal Building, June 11, 1951. (HBM&S)

Martha Cressey and Post Master Don Craig. (Reminder)

Theresa 'Chickie' Iannone, first Queen Mermaid, July 1951. (Trout Festival)

Roy 'Baldy' Jackson and Orris Sage winners of the first Gold Rush 125 mile Canoe Race, July 1951. (Trout Festival)

Queen Mermaid Tea. (Joan Edwards)

Junior Prospector's Race during Trout Festival. (Reminder)

Trout Festival Parade, June 30, 1952. (Trout Festival)

Gwen Miller, Queen, with Princesses Eleanor Kepper and Doreen Anderson; Cliff McKay and Bud Jobin, 1952. (Man. Gov't. Travel and Publicity Bureau)

The first telephone building was erected in 1938. (MTS)

The present Manitoba Telephone Building was erected in 1952 at the corner of Third and Ross. (MTS)

Glee Club production of 'The Gondoliers' in 1952 was produced by Ron Price. (J. E. Goodman)

'The Gondaliers'. (J. E. Goodman)

Christmas Concert by the Glee Club, 1952. (J. E. Goodman)

No. 302 Air Cadet Squadron 'Wings Parade', February 20, 1952. (HBM&S)

Queen Elizabeth II Coronation Parade, June 1953 — Royal Coach. (HBM&S)

Royal Coach with 'Queen and Beef Eater'. (HBM&S)

Canadian Legion Float followed the Royal Coach. (HBM&S)

Rotary Club entry. (HBM&S)

B.P.O. Elks (E. Runehjelm)

Order of Royal Purple. (HBM&S)

Chinese Citizens Float, June 1953. (E. Runehjelm)

Chinese Float. (HBM&S)

Comic Float. (HBM&S)

Brownies Float. (HBM&S)

Brownies and Guides at Phantom Lake, June 1953. (HBM&S)

Cubs and Scouts at Phantom Lake, June 1953. (HBM&S)

Willowvale School Museum, 1952. (HBM&S)

Willowvale School addition, 1952. (HBM&S)

Hudson School was built in 1954. (Reminder)

1953 Graduation Class. (Reminder)

East side of Hudson School, 1954. (Reminder)

Janet Wood at the Arena, 1953. (HBM&S)

Legion Ladies' Auxiliary 20th Anniversary, 1953. Left to right — Ada Norquay, Beatrice Davies, Julia Routlege, Myrtle Longmore, Cathy VanderWal, Florence McGinnis. (Legion)

Lena O'Neal's Ballet Class, 1953-54. (HBM&S)

Ballet Class. (HBM&S)

14th Annual Rotary Carnival, August 1954. Left to right — Bill Sonnichsen, Lew Parres, Jim Fetterly and Doug McBride. (Reminder)

14th Annual Rotary Carnival and Horticultural Show, August 1954. Myrtice Strand, Queen, Princesses — Ruth Ann Cyr, Sheila Emery, Enid Delgatty and Marilyn Keddie. (Reminder)

Jack Freedman, Mayor 1953 to 1956. (J. Gilmore)

Mayor Freedman's 'Fall In'. (Reminder)

Mayor Freedman opens Cordwood Bonspiel. (Reminder)

Mayor Freedman presents trophy to Flin Flon Bombers. (Reminder)

Left to right: Art Hildebrand, Otto Bergman Royal Bank Manager and Dennis Crossman Accountant. (Royal Bank 1954)

Mayor Freedman and Chamber of Commerce members making a 'clean sweep'. Left to right: Sam Hankin, Mayor Freedman, John Wilson, Bill Sonnichsen and Fred Kyba. (Reminder 1955)

Northern Echoes was formed by Pete Stevenson on right. (Reminder 1955)

Teen Canteen Orchestra during the 1950's. (Reminder)

Northminster United Church Junior Choir, 1956. Left to right, Back Row: Gail Wardle, Gail Buchanon, Gail Parsons, Wilma Uhrich, Betty McAree, Margaret Delgatty, Marjorie Hall. Middle Row: Bonnie Hutchinson, Gail Lawrence, Joan Buchanon, Carol Webb, Barbara Biggs, Faye Thompson. Front Row: Joan McKague, Norma Berry, Karen Gadd, Jeanette Odegaard. (Marjorie Hall)

Lutheran Church Junior Choir. (HBM&S)

Members of the Lutheran Church burning the mortgage on the building at 50 Hill Street. (HBM&S)

Maurice A. Roche, one of the few northern Canadians to receive Knighthood in the Order of St. Gregory The Great, May 16, 1954. (Jim Callin)

Mrs. Roche, Sir Maurice Roche and His Excellency Bishop Martin Lajeunesse, OMI, DD, May 16, 1954. (Jim Callin)

Scaffolding on St. George's Ukrainian Church, 1953. (Reminder)

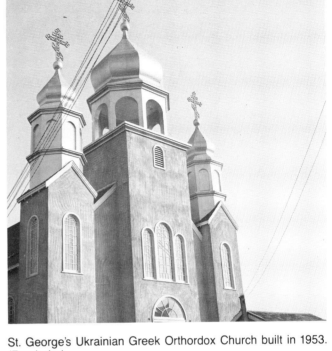

St. George's Ukrainian Greek Orthordox Church built in 1953. (Reminder)

Easter service at St. George's, 1953. (Reminder)

St. Andrew's Presbyterian Church dedicated May 1954. (Reminder)

Laying the cornerstone for St. Andrew's, 1954. (Reminder)

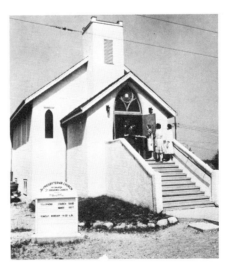

St. Andrew's, 1954. (St. Andrew's)

Town Public Works and Utilities prepare for sewer and water in east Birchview with Mayor Freedman turning first shovel of dirt. Looking on are Andy Watson, Dick Evans, Charlie Hagen, Ernie Ransom, Bob Comstock and Henry Hartle, July 26, 1955. (Reminder)

Flood at Main and First Avenue, 1954. (Reminder)

The arch was erect in 1955 by John Highmoor. (Reminder)

Lakeside bridge caused many problems, 1952. (Reminder)

Removing hill on First Avenue. (Reminder)

Opening of the Lion's Club Safety Lane, June 24, 1955. (Reminder)

Channing Wolverines, 1951. Left to right, Front Row: Virginia Smith, Noreen Paquette, Helen Vancoughnett, Lyle Anderson, Gloria Vancoughnett, Donna Emery. Back Row: Sheila Emery, Nina Alquire, Merle Wurtack, Elsie Dowhan, Sylvia Davie, Eileen Emery. (Donna Chev)

Cardinals won Polar League Championship in 1956. (Jack Greenberg)

Kopper Kweens, 1955. Some players are: Monica Vickery, Angie Plaiash, Gail Hampson, Gay Bogash, Mary Mason, Martha McKenzie and Wanda Leary. (Reminder)

Ladies of the Uptown Curling Club. Left to right, Front Row: Audrey McNabb, Joan Howatt, Bernice Monson, Marg McBratney, Tina Konik. Back Row: Annie McIntosh, Bertha Schneider, Smitty Austin, Nel Hutchinson and Monica Donald. (Reminder)

Winners of the Western Curling Championship sponsored by Eatons. Left to right: Ethel Wright, Norma McLean, Jean McKenzie and Philomene Floch, Spring 1955. (Reminder)

Life members of the Flin Flon Curling Club, February 1954. Left to right: Jock Thomson, Roy Diamond, Jack McDonald, Sam Hankin, W. A. Green, Harold Stevens, George Murton and Ole Wick. (HBM&S)

Legion Convention — saluting base, June 1955. (W. S. B. Lockhart)

(HBM&S)

Legion Convention — Main Street, June 1955. (Reminder)

Official opening of the addition to the upstairs of the Legion Hall. Charter member Cap Gilbertson cuts official ribbon, April 1958. (HBM&S)

W. S. B. Lockhart and Jim Wardle opening of the upstairs of the Legion Hall. (HBM&S)

Commissioner Ruth McPherson and Beth Thompson with Gold Cord Guides — Kathleen Houston, Anne Sabo, Cecile Gira, Bernice Burgess, Pat Douglas, Donela Holdaway, Mary Dubrack and Gail Lockhart, Fall 1954. (Reminder)

Barbara Jean Killoh receives her Gold Cord from Miss Marjorie Hoskins, Spring 1955. (HBM&S)

Brownie Pack No. 1 were winners of the Nasselquist Trophy for Folk Songs. (D. K. Ash)

Guides honor Mrs. Cal Huntley with a 25 Year Thank You Pin presented by Miss M. Hoskins, February 7, 1955. (Reminder)

Mothers and Daughters in Guiding — Houston, Greenberg and Pickworth. (Reminder)

Lady Baden-Powell in Flin Flon shakes hands with Brownies, September 1955. (Reminder)

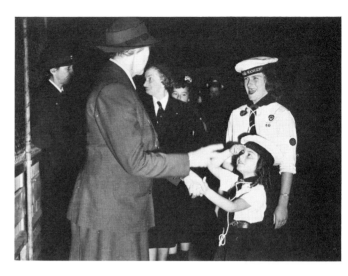

Rangers. (Reminder)

Gold Cord Guides. (Reminder)

Cub Scouts. (Reminder)

Grand welcome for Lady Baden-Powell in the Arena. (Reminder)

Farewell. (Reminder)

Girl Guides receive $500 from Swift's, January 1956. (Girl Guides)

Rangers Pat Merrell, Alayne Wright and Helen Booth receive Gold Cords from Mrs. W. J. Riley, Provincial Commissioner. Back Row: Kay Huntley, Beth Thompson District Commissioner East, Marg Smith and Ruth McPherson Division Commissioner, 1957. (Girl Guides)

Ranger enrollment, February 1957. (HBM&S)

Pack 9B Brownies with 'Ditty Bags' for Korea. (Ruth Shomperlen)

Girl Guides Association, Margaret Hartman, Phyl Smith, Vi Kirkwood and Doris Holmes. (Ruth Shomperlen)

2nd Troop Boy Scouts: Gord Stevenson, Gord Smith, Hugh McBratney, Hank Drennan, Reg McInnis, H. Bergstrom, Merle Jackson, Frank Norquay, Gordon Kitchen, Alistair Campbell, Walter Bowes, Jack Noble, Neil McLennan, Fred Ford, George Avison, Don McRae, Gordon Waldmo, Ernie Peterson, George Ostry, Gray Brothers and G. Feldman. (M. McBratney)

Ron Dodge presents a cheque to Bob Davison and leading Scouts who were attending the 8th World Jamboree in England, Summer 1957. (HBM&S)

Apple Day. (Reminder)

Cubs waiting at the siding for the train to bring them back from Camp Whitney. (George Struch)

Bath Day at Camp Whitney for the Cubs. (George Struch)

Sam Hankin was appointed Badge Secretary of the Boy Scouts' Organization in March 1942. Over 300 proficiency badges were given out in 1958. (HBM&S)

Corona Hotel Fire, December 6, 1955. (Reminder)

Dr. B. A. Biggs lost his office in the hotel fire. (Reminder)

Left to right: Cliff Clarke, Fire Chief Walter Redman and Albert Pogue. (Reminder)

Bob Gray 'The pause that refreshes'. (Reminder)

Fire Prevention Week at Birchview School, October 1956. (Reminder)

Fire Chief Redman talks to the pupils of Birchview School, October 1956. (Reminder)

Robbie Burns' Night, January 1956, Peter McSheffrey reads the toast to the Haggis. (Reminder)

Lion L's help out with the Lions' Club Radio Auction, 1956. (Reminder)

Club 27, 25th annual celebration, December 1, 1956. Left to right, Standing Back Row: Bill Grayson, Art Pickworth, W. A. Green, Algot Mosell, Tom Barker, Ed Hagen, Harry Guymer, Dean Smith, Ole Hagen, Frank Gummerson, Bill Barker, M. A. Roche, James Thompson, D. B. McGilvray. Standing Front Row: James Bell, Peter Maloney, Albert Reaney, George Winterton, Fred Hollier, Jack Floch, Ralph Bloomfield, Tom Lamb, Sid Hudson. Seated Back Row: Arnie Akert, Irene Green, Jean Lamb, Louise Hone, Isabelle Akert, Iver Heggmark, Bill Hughes. Seated Front Row: Eugene Germain, Glen Rapson, Jack Hone, Jacob Steinarson, George Jones. (Flin Flon 27 Club)

D. K. Ash, winner of Manitoba Provincial Scholarship to Banff School of Fine Arts, 1956. (D. K. Ash)

George and Bernard Ostry. (Archives)

Jack Greenberg sharpened skates at the Arena. (Reminder 1956)

Art Wahlenberg with pet owl. (Reminder 1956)

Sam Rumbal, Rotary Horticultural Exhibition. (Reminder)

Harry Lofendale (Santa) visits the Clinic to exchange gifts. (Reminder)

The Armouries opened in November 1956. (HBM&S)

Armouries. (Reminder)

Army on parade for the official opening of the Armouries. (Reminder)

Navy Cadets are inspected by Commander Penfold, 1953. (Reminder)

Navy Cadets take in a movie. (Reminder)

RCSCC Husky Navy Cadets, 1955. (Reminder)

Camp Comox, 1954 — Brad Sexsmith, Charles Ciprick, Dave Duffner, Glenn Anderson, Ed Barr, Marvin Dowhan and Instructor Wilson. (G. Kramer)

Left to right: Wayne Mawby, Allan Fidler, Don Wilkes and Calvin Christianson, at Junior Leaders' Course held at Clear Lake Army Cadet Camp, August 8, 1960. (Reminder)

Air Cadets, 1954. (HBM&S)

Wings to D. Balfour and T. McFadden (front row). Back Row, left to right: Cpl. W. Hanna, Jr. Rifle Competition; AC2 R. Bernard, 1st Year Cadet Trophy; WO2 D. Ricard, Efficiency Shield and Flying Training; AC2 R. Stoltz, Senior Rifle Competition. (Reminder)

Sword presented to Lieut. Glen Kramer when RCSCC Husky won Junior Proficiency Trophy for Canada in 1957. Left to right: Glen Kramer, John Lucas, Charlie Dickens, Len Pickell and Forest Green. (HBM&S)

Navy Cadets, Christmas, 1958. (HBM&S)

Abbott Cup Champs welcomed home, 1957. (Reminder)

Memorial Cup Champions, May 1957. (Reminder)

Flin Flon Bombers Welcome Home, 1957. (Reminder)

Passing the time until the Community Hall ticket office opened for Memorial Cup Games, 1957. (Reminder)

Memorial Cup Winners — Flin Flon Bombers, 1957. (Reminder)

John Diefenbaker visits Flin Flon, May 1957 to offer congratulations to the Bombers. (Reminder)

FLIN FLON JUNIOR BOMBERS
Canadian Junior Hockey Champions 1956-57

WINNERS OF THE MEMORIAL CHALLENGE CUP FOR CANADIAN CHAMPIONSHIP ... THE ABBOTT MEMORIAL
CUP FOR WESTERN CANADA CHAMPIONSHIP ... THE CORBEAU CUP FOR SASKATCHEWAN
CHAMPIONSHIP ... THE ROBIN HOOD TROPHY FOR NORTHERN SASKATCHEWAN CHAMPIONSHIP

MEMORIAL CHALLENGE CUP

ORLAND KURTENBACH
FORWARD

WAYNE SPROXTON
FORWARD

ROD LEE
FORWARD

CARL FORSTER
FORWARD

CLIFF LENNARTZ
FORWARD

MEL PEARSON
FORWARD

ABBOTT MEMORIAL CUP

PAT GINNELL
FORWARD

HARVEY FLEMING
FORWARD

BARRY BEATTY
FORWARD

RON HUTCHINSON
FORWARD

JEAN GAUTHIER
DEFENCE

MIKE KARDASH
DEFENCE

GEORGE KONIK
DEFENCE

DUANE RUPP
DEFENCE

KEN WILLEY
DEFENCE

LYNN DAVIS
GOAL

GEORGE WOOD
GOAL

TED HAMPSON
CAPTAIN

BUD SIMPSON
EXECUTIVE

DOUG DAWSON
MANAGER

BOB KIRK
COACH

HEC McCAIG
TRAINER

JIM WARDLE
EXECUTIVE

REESE JONES AND KEN CUNNINGHAM
STICK BOYS

CORBEAU CUP

ALEC HRYN
EXECUTIVE

SLIM HOLDAWAY
EXECUTIVE

LEN LAVITT
EXECUTIVE

PINKY DAVIE
EXECUTIVE

HARVEY McNICHOL M.D.
CLUB DOCTOR

ROBIN HOOD TROPHY

(Hec McCaig)

117

F. L. Jobin, Minister of Industry and Commerce for the Liberal Party of Manitoba, 1953 to 1958. Donni, Onalee and Bud. (Reminder)

Kay and Bud Simpson — first victory as a Progressive Conservative Member in the Churchill Constituency, 1957. (Reminder)

C. H. 'Buck' Witney, Manager of Radio Station CFAR (1949-1959) was elected member to the Progressive Conservative Provincial Government in 1959. (Davidson Studios)

Left to right: Cyril Steventon, Norma Tissot and Mayor Frank Dembinsky, May 1957. (HBM&S)

Rotary Carnival, August 1957. Left to right: Princess Ann Inglefield, Queen Kathy Cheveldaeff, Princesses Shirley Jesperson and Evelyn Stevenson. (Donna Chev)

Rotary Queen Heather McDougall, Princesses Deena Henry, Dodie Martin, Ruth Feldman and Karen Baily. Pages Barbara McKay and Grace Ruse, 1958. (Reminder)

Royal Court of 1959. (Reminder)

Kids Serkus, August 30, 1958. Princesses Celia Kemp, Sonia Thiele, Margaret Lengyel, Agnes Beilby, Joine Martin, Linda McCutcheon. Queen Diane Woloshyn crowned by Eric Runehjelm. (Reminder)

Kids Serkus Queen Karen Johannson and her Court. Left to right: Valerie Gutenberg, Laurel Lofgren, Barbara Smith, Marjorie Cree, Sandra Sangster, Linda McLean, Myfawny Crerar and Shirly Langlois, August 31, 1960. (Reminder)

Karen Wiig, Trout Festival Queen, 1956. (Trout Festival)

Scotch Dancers on Main Street, 1957. (Bureau of Travel & Publicity)

Dominion Day Bathing Beauties, 1957. (Bureau of Travel & Publicity)

Trout Festival Queen, Leola St. Godard, 1957. (Bureau of Travel & Publicity)

Best Dressed Doll Contest in one of the Trout Festivals. (HBM&S)

St. Peter's Anglican Church — cornerstone was laid June 6, 1955. (HBM&S)

Rev. Murray Ames of St. Peter's with the Hume family. Thelma Hume (front) conducted 'Kiddies Club' over CFAR from February 1954 until late in 1967. (Hume 1959)

First Baptist Church. (Val Hedman)

Opening of the Salvation Army Citadel, January 9, 1959. Left to right: Major Sharp, Commissioner Booth, Mrs. Carey and Captain Carey. (Reminder)

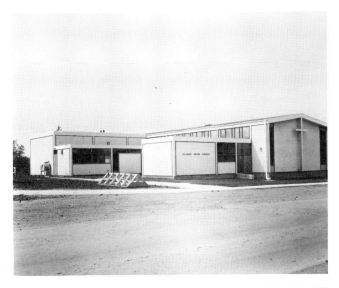

St. Luke's United Church was dedicated October 20, 1957. (Reminder)

St. James' Anglican Church addition opened October 26, 1961. (St. James)

St. Paul's Catholic Church under construction, 1956. (Reminder)

Cornerstone to St. Paul's was laid in 1956. (Reminder)

Bishop Dumouchel blessed St. Paul's on March 11, 1957. (HBM&S)

Most Reverend Paul Dumouchel, Maurice Baudoux DD and P. F. Pocock with Sir Maurice Roche and Lady Enid Roche at official opening of Sir Maurice Roche School, 1959. (Sir Maurice Roche School)

Sir Maurice Roche High School, 1958. (Sir Maurice Roche School)

Trout Festival Queen Evelyn Geyson with Bob Ash, Bud Simpson and a 38 pound lake trout, 1958. (Trout Festival)

Street Fair at the Trout Festival, 1958. (Trout Festival)

Trout Festival Executive. Some members were: Bob Ash, Jim Conner, Bob Dadson, Keith Taylor, Peter McSheffrey, Joe Pico and Otto Bergman. (HBM&S)

Community Hall was built in 1957-1958. (HBM&S)

Mayor Frank Dembinsky officially opened the Community Hall, February 1958. (HBM&S)

Official opening of the Community Hall with the Pipe Band in attendance. (Reminder)

Arnie Akert retirement, June 1958. Left to right, Back Row: Maurice Smith, Dick Mainwaring, Hal Roberts, Bob Maguire, Gordon Donogh, Glen Campbell, Harry Grose, Cal Huntley, Emery Switzer, Wilf Watt, Bill Vatcher, Ken Klause, Doug Ross, Frank Bocklage. Front Row: Jim Foley, Mike Nowazek, Eddie Martin, Don Fryer, Arnie Akert, Dorothy Linden, Tom Warren, Seth Matthews, Wes Vickery, Frank Schneider. (Reminder)

Marilyn Keddie, Miss Maple Leaf, September 1958. (Adrian Photography)

Northern Bus Line employees on strike, February 1969. (Reminder)

Newly formed Bus Line. Left to right: Jack Ross, Mayor Frank Dembinsky, Councillors Eric Runehjelm and Alex Chisholm, November 20, 1959. (Reminder)

Fruit and Produce Fire, July 8, 1959. (Bob Bryson)

COOP Garage — Manager Joe Griffith holds award. Left to right: Don Crone, Sanford Ernest, Joe Griffith, Mr. Tall, Bill Reader, Bob Ewen, June 9, 1960. (Archives)

Post Office Christmas mail, December 1958. (Reminder)

Cenotaph unveiled August 9, 1959. (Legion)

Parade of Legion members past Cenotaph, 1959. (Legion)

Mrs. J. McCormick laid wreath for Silver Star Mothers, August 1959. (Legion)

Mayor Frank Dembinsky laid wreath for the Town of Flin Flon, 1959. (Legion)

Bicycle Safety at the Main School playground, 1959. (Reminder)

Aqua Lung Divers, Tony Csapo, Cal Bevins and Boots Nomeland, July 1958. (Reminder)

Hapnot students took over the Town on May 17, 1960. Youth Week Mayor Edna Fisher surrounded by Sharon Hopkinson, Clerk and Councillors Fred Robinson, Al Marshall, Bob McKenzie, Paul Neilson, Del Tusz and Ray Huntley. (Reminder)

Louis Martel tests one of the new karts belonging to the Kart Klub, August 15, 1960. (Reminder)

Sylvan Kart Track officially opened September 11, 1961. (Reminder)

Mayor Dembinsky cuts the ribbon to officially open the artificial ice curling rink 'Willowpark', November 10, 1960. In attendance were Bud Jobin, Sid Brown, Eric Austin, Jim Robertson and Bud Simpson. (Reminder)

'Order of the Buffalo' presented to the Isabelle Ketchen Rink for capturing the Western Canada Eaton Curling Championships, May 12, 1959. Left to right: Hon. Jack Carroll, Isabelle Ketchen, Doris McFarlane, Isabelle Phillips, Ruth McConnell and Bud Jobin. (Reminder)

Flo McInnes and her Ross Lake Rink captured the Grand Aggregate Honors in the Ladies' Bonspiel February 1960. Left to right: Flo McInnes, Edna Hopkinson, Jean Hook and Sadie George. (Reminder)

Joy Longmore and Flo McInnes, 1960. (Reminder)

Remember the Two Bit Bonspiel of February 1961? (Reminder)

Reminder and the Post Office fight over the coveted CFAR 'CUP', 1961. (Reminder)

Opening ceremonies in the Whitney Forum, October 15, 1960. (Reminder)

Bud Jobin unveils plaque which reads: This arena is today named Whitney Forum by the Flin Flon Community Club in Appreciation of the donation of the building by Hudson Bay Mining & Smelting Co., Limited, October 15, 1960. (Reminder)

Smelter Midgets, Hammy Benson, Coach and Tommy Leel, Assistant Coach, 1960. (HBM&S)

Kinsmen Midgets, 1960. (HBM&S)

Elks Midget Hockey Team, 1960. (HBM&S)

Legion Midget Team, Bill Maluta, Coach and Ken Huffman, Manager, 1960. (HBM&S)

Flin Flon Rotary Flyers Midget Hockey Team, 1960. (HBM&S)

Ostry's Midget Team, 1960. (HBM&S)

Flin Flon Fire Department Midget Team, 1960. (HBM&S)

Dog House Midget Team, 1960. (HBM&S)

Schieders Midget Team receive the trophy from Orville Thompson, 1960. (HBM&S)

Hockey Press Club, November 7, 1961. Left to right: Bud Killick, Bruce Keddie, Jim Wardle and Carl Edmonds. (Reminder)

130

25-year appreciation for Dr. and Mrs. Johnson, September 18, 1960. Left to right: George Komanac, Dr. Percy Johnson, Elizabeth Johnson and Dorothy Milton. (Reminder)

Knights of Columbus presented cheques to the General Hospital and Sir Maurice Roche School, October 24, 1961. Left to right: Charlie Mahoney, Frank Gira, Arnold Stephansson, Nick Iannone. Front Row: Sister Dion, Father Sullivan and Sister Remillard. (Reminder)

Rev. Murray Ames, President of the local Mental Health Association and Mayor Frank Dembinsky, hold the award presented to Flin Flon by the Mental Health Association for outstanding contributions in 1959. (Reminder)

Vi Coombs, President of the United Church Ladies' Auxiliary received a gift of cutlery from Rotarian Bal Biggs in appreciation of the many luncheons provided by the ladies, December 1960. (Reminder)

Kinsmen School was officially opened November 19, 1960. (Reminder)

Del Johnson, President of the Kinsmen Club presented the keys to the school, along with a scroll, to Dorothy Linden, President of the A.R.C., November 19, 1960. (Reminder)

Ukrainian Women's League of St. George's Church, 1960. Front Row, left to right: Mesdames, H. Stratychuk, F. Maluta, J. Storozuk, W. Skwarchuk, A. Aponiuk, M. Jankovich, J. Puritch, G. Prochuk, P. Mendro. Middle Row: M. Crapan, A. Chocholik, A. Znamanchuk, S. Olineck, N. Andrychuk, W. Perepeluk, F. Smorhay, S. Danyluk, A. Dobrahorsky. Third Row: N. Dolinsky, N. Klewchuk, M. Todaschuk, F. Kyba, P. Skwarchuk, J. Klewchuk, J. Dolinsky, S. Yacentiuk, M. Klewchuk, B. Newransky. (HBM&S)

Lion's Club Radio Auction, CFAR — November 26, 1960. Left to right: Tony Samolesky, Lloyd Duncanson, Larry Hall and Don Craig. (Reminder)

Florrie Howell presented a cheque on behalf of the Eastern Star to Rotary President Bill Sonnichsen to be used for landscaping Rotary Court, December 17, 1960. (Reminder)

Howie Shiffman tries out one of the cars in the Kin Kar Derby. Executive left to right: Art Opheium, Jack Steventon, Bill Robillard, Ted Wright, Dick Berthiaume and Jack Shiffman, 1960. (Reminder)

Kinsmen Variety Show, February 3, 1960, featuring Misses "Satchi" Sachkiw, Doni Donaldson and Charlette Mahoney. (Reminder)

Don Nisbet and Barbara Fraser receive Legion Bursaries from Lillian Genovy, September 9, 1961. (Reminder)

Legion Auxiliary presented mops, pails, etc., to Rotary Court. Left to right: B. Thompson, Nels Grant, Mrs. I. Pockett, Lil Genovy, Mrs. M. Sizer and Helen Lawton, January 13, 1961. (Reminder)

Legion sponsored Sports Training. Left to right: George Phillips, Pat Wullum, Violet Wands and Fred Taylor, July 1961. (Reminder)

Carol Donaldson was the winner of the Governor General's Award presented by Principal J. B. Kines, May 27, 1960. (Reminder)

Hapnot Collegiate Awards. Left to right, Back Row: Glen Duncan, Arthur Thom, Tom Javorsky, Fred Robertson. Front Row: Donald Morrison, Bob Forsyth, Alfred Wikjord, May 27, 1960. (Reminder)

Major Awards at Hapnot High, May 27, 1960. Left to right: Beverley Joyce, Sharon Hopkinson, Adele Ulinder, Thelma Davies and Karen Gadd. (Reminder)

133

Mayor Frank Dembinsky hits the first ball of the season, June 3, 1960. (Reminder)

Ross Lake Bantam Club, June 15, 1960. (Reminder)

Hapnot High Freshies and Cheer Leaders, October 6, 1960. (Reminder)

Creighton Ladies' Fastball Team with the lastest in 'Hat Fashions', October 1961. (Reminder)

Birchview Braves Bantam Champs, Captain Allan Donogh, 1966. (Reminder)

Flin Flon Soccer Club, Northern Soccer League Pennant winners, September 17, 1962. Left to right, Back Row: Carl Baver, Hank Beck, Jack Higgs, Adolf Kauss, Alfred Kauss, Fabian Wong, Frank Warning, Timmy Szonolany, George Sey (Coach). Front Row: Remo Beck, John Verkierk, George Kohut, Steve Bortos, Henry Heideveld. (Reminder)

Official opening of Rotary Court, February 10, 1961. Left to right: Bill Sonnichsen (Rotary President), Hon. George Johnson (Minister of Health), Dr. Malcolmson (cutting ribbon), George Evans (Chairman), and Hon. C. H. Witney (Minister of Mines). (Reminder)

Rotary Court, 1961. (Reminder)

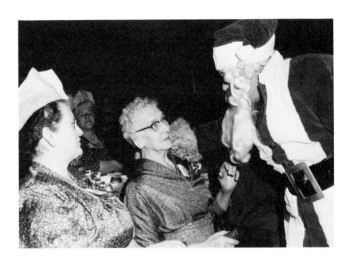

Residents of Rotary Court, August 16, 1961 at a farewell party for Mr. and Mrs. Charlie Britten. (Reminder)

Senior Citizen's Christmas Party, December 13, 1960. Left to right: A. McIntosh, I. Bowes, N. Hutchinson and Santa. (Reminder)

Erecting the Christmas Tree on Main Street, early 1960's. (Reminder)

All set. (Reminder)

Knights of Columbus. Left to right, Front Row: Serge Richer, Ed Gardewine, Joe Prendeville, John Zoretich, Leo Soen, Modestieno Iannone, Bernard Reagen, Norm Stephansson. Back Row: Ray Gibney, Allen Pollmeier, Allen Marshall, Arnold Stephansson, Charlie Mahoney, Jim Campbell, Joe Czettisch, Andy Gutenberg, 1961-1962. (Knights of Columbus)

First United Lutheran Church, 1961. (Val Hedman)

Cornerstone of the Lutheran Church was laid July 30, 1961 and the Church dedicated December 3, 1961. (Reminder)

Flin Flon Fire Department, March 1961. Left to right, Back Row: B. Figas, A. Maloney, G. Nolgren, D. Still, E. Stevenson, C. Dickens, D. Leach, K. McKee, A. Deans, J. Larsson, R. Hagen, A. Chlan. Centre Row: D. McLaren, M. Stonehouse, C. Jones, W. Miller, B. Smale, J. Coulthard, F. Berry, J. Doan, K. Burr, N. McKenzie. Front Row: S. Smith, M. Garuk, D. Gourlay, A. Pogue, F. Livesey, Chief Redman, C. Clarke, F. Roy, W. McFadden, W. Andres. (Flin Flon Fire Department)

Mr. and Mrs. Walter Redman on their departure from Flin Flon, April 1961. (Reminder)

The Volunteer Firemen presented a cheque to Captain Ed Reed of the Salvation Army. Left to right: Captain Reed, A. Pogue, Fire Chief Livesey and Earl Steven, March 24, 1962. (Reminder)

Mayor and Mrs. Jack Freedman take in a local hockey game. (Reminder)

Mayor Jack Freedman and Creighton's Mayor Alex Clark, November 26, 1962. (Reminder)

Councillor Dorothy Milton brought greetings from the Town of Flin Flon, August 3, 1960; with her is Hon. Alex Muzial, Minister of Saskatchewan Natural Resources. (Reminder)

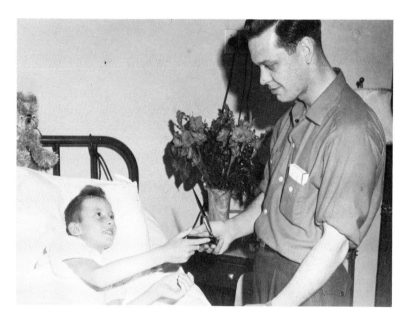

Harvey Evans is presented with a token of thanks from Walter Sedor, spring 1960. (Reminder)

George Murton's retirement from the Town. Left to right: George Mainwaring, George Murton, George Evans and Frank Dembinsky, 1962. (City of Flin Flon)

Tribute for thirty years service to the Town was presented to George Evans. Left to right: Sandy Morrice, Gus McMillan, George Evans, Jim Conner, Herman McKinnon and Doug Evans, June 1963. (Reminder)

Girl Guides planted tulips in Rotary Park to celebrate 50 years of Guiding in Canada, 1960. (Ruth Shomperlen)

Tulips were also planted in Willowvale, 1960. (R. Shomperlen)

Past District Commissioner Noreen Watson congratulated Betty Hopkins upon receiving her Gold Cord, December 1964. (Reminder)

Gold Cords were also presented to Pat Folwark (left) and Judy Maitland (right) by Ruth Shomperlen, Commissioner, December 1964. (R. Shomperlen)

Legion President Al Anderson presented a cheque to District Commissioner Norm Murphy to help with the upkeep of the Scout Hall, November 1962. (Reminder)

Doug Ormiston (right), President of Lions' Club, turned over the deed to the Lutheran Church building (50 Hill) to Dr. Glen Willson, President of the Scout Association, November 1964. (Reminder)

Pat Donaghy, organizer of the opening day 'Flypast' for 503 (Wing) RCAF welcomes the 'Red Knight', May 26, 1962. (Reminder)

To officially open a segment of the airport a cable stretched across the runway was cut by the prop of Steve Olench's plane, 1962. (Reminder)

Bob Ferguson added some comedy to the Flypast, May 26, 1962. (Reminder)

(Reminder)

C. H. Witney (centre) officially opened the 'Kelsey Trail'. With him are Ray Mullaney (with sign) and Dave Robertson (right), 1964. (Reminder)

Left to right: Tony Samolesky, Bud Jobin, Ray Mullaney, Howard McIntosh and Carl Edmonds, 1964. (Reminder)

503 (Wing) RCAF, hosted Manitoba and Northwestern Ontario Command Convention in Flin Flon, March 1964. (Edgar Grandison)

302 Squadron RCAF, 1962. Left to right, Back Row: Dennis Anderson, Percy Callin, Joe McCormick, Bob Jarvis, Gordon Wooley. Front Row: Malcolm Ferguson, Danny Woronuik, Gord McKenzie, Don Harland, Stan Cox, Jack Willis, Nick Oklobdzija, Allan Row, Keith Staszko, Rick Alexander. (302 Squadron)

Jim Conner, Mayor of Flin Flon, 1963 and 1964. (J. Conner)

Game and Fish Association Executive, 1962. Left to right: Charlie Nelson, Dollard Heurie, Irwin Drinkwater, Johnny McKay, Roy Mast, Ken Radford, Gordon Doverspike, Reg Luchuck, Jim Lambkin, Pat Ferg, Eunice Nelson, Roy Switzer, Bob Ferguson. (Reminder)

Chamber of Commerce with some that didn't get away. Left to right: Steve Kowalewich, Fred Maluta, Bob Hiscox, Mickey Perepeluk, Leif Reitlo, Alf Boyce, Ray Hicken, 1960's. (Reminder)

Chamber of Commerce Fishing Derby, August 1960. Left to right: Bruce Keddie, Ted Keddie, Bill Keddie and Steve Andrusiak. (Reminder)

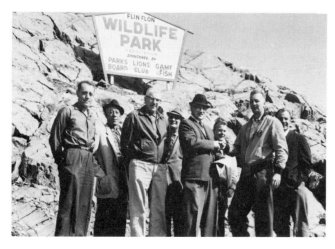

Left to right: Albert Feldmann, Roy Mast, George Emerson, Harry Lofendale, Allan Pollmeier, Ivor Hedman, Lloyd Wright, Pat Ferg, 1964. (Reminder)

Lawrence Hamilton — feeding time at Wildlife Park, Hapnot Lake Sanctuary, 1960's. (Reminder)

Gold Rush Canoe winners, July 1965. Left to right: Gib McEachern, Labatt's representative with trophy, and Norm Crerar. (Trout Festival)

Trout Festival Executive, 1964. Left to right, Back Row: John McKay, Stan Curtis, Otto Bergman, Colin Harrell, Joe Pico. Centre Row: Fred Ford, Keith Taylor, Bud Jobin, Tony Samolesky, Bill Folwark. Front Row: Joni Hammerstad, Carl Edmonds, Marg Smith. (Joe Pico)

Flour packing — 700 pounds, Trout Festival, 1962. (Trout Festival)

Jigging contest Beaver Lake Day, 1962. (Trout Festival)

Manitoba School Boy Championship participants leave to play in the Dominion Finals, January 1962. Left to right: Bob Green lead, Tom Longmore second, Al Hume third and Jim Willox skip. (Reminder)

Winners of the Burkett Event, Ladies' Bonspiel, March 1964. Left to right: Wilma Gallagher, Tina Konik, Beatty Byers and Joyce Trueman. (Reminder)

Cordwood Bonspiel winners, April 1963. Left to right: Del Iannone, Stephen Dembinsky, Dana Row and Ron Danyluk. (Reminder)

1966 Cordwood Bonspiel. Left to right: Jack Willey, Ken Scott, Ray Maluta and Wayne Scott. (Reminder)

Main Event winners in Badminton, 1964. Left to right: Ken Rusk, Adaline Rheaume, Fred Burton, Anne McGrath, Diane Grayson. (Campbell's)

Badminton, 1964. Left to right: Bev Dougall, Tony McDonald, Al McGrath, Fred Burton, Gerry Dougall and Anne McGrath. (Campbell's)

Perepeluk family. Left to right: John, Bill and Mickey, 1960's. (Reminder)

Frank Schieder, 1969. (Campbell's)

James Lister, 1964. (Reminder)

Harry Moody. (Trout Festival)

Ted Olson and his Seeing Eye Dog 'Lady', December 1967. (Reminder)

Plaque erected to Harry Moody's historic artifacts discovered in the Amisk Lake area, 1967. (Reminder)

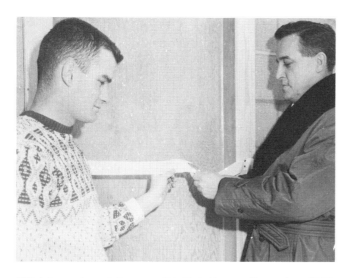

Official opening of the new Ski Club House, December, 1960, by Bud Quinnell and Bud Jobin. (Reminder)

Some of the local skiers, January 1962. (Reminder)

Left to right: David Crerar, Bob McNeil, Norm Crerar and Phil MacLellan, 1962. (Bud Quinnell)

Tom Baird and Joe Gurba, owners of the Putt-A-Round, add finishing touches prior to opening August 4, 1962. (Reminder)

John Akert, winner of the Phantom Lake Golf Club Championship, August 1964, presented with trophy by Arnold 'Zeke' Nowosad. (Al Warrington)

Tee Time for Fred Burton, while Dr. Peter Premachuk, Milt Young, Jim Russell and Caddy Premachuk wait their turn, 1966. (Reminder)

Official ribbon cutting at Ruth Betts School, February 21, 1964. (Reminder)

Superintendent of Schools, Ivan Hamilton presents scrolls to Mrs. Helen McKenzie and Mrs. W. I. Stewart, sisters of Ruth Betts, 1964. (Reminder)

Graduates of a Hapnot Home and School sponsored course in Service Station Attendants, April 1966. Stan Soltyz (right centre) presents certificate to graduate Ron Dickson while Carson McAdoo (centre) looks on. (Reminder)

Seven young ladies enrolled in an economic course offered by the School Association. Evelyn Black (left) and Elizabeth Genik (right) were the instructors, April 1966. (Reminder)

Senior High Most Valuable Basketball Players. Left to right: Bill McDonald, Angie Kowal and Bob Toal, June 1966. (Reminder)

Junior High Basketball Championship. Left to right: Don Zachinack, Ed Kluba, Dennis Nowroski, Ray Martyniuk, Tony Smida, June 1966. (Reminder)

Royal Bank Building. (Royal Bank)

Royal Bank staff, 1964. Left to right, Back Row: Trudy Linnick, Bernice Gourlay, Addie Banting, Joan Thorley, Gail Lomax, Karen Rachuck, Diane Grayson. Front Row: Darla Prier, Grace Lethbridge, Judie Pettapiece, Linda McLean, Lynne Hagberg. (Joan Thorley)

Fire at the Royal Hotel, January 27, 1966. (Reminder)

Flin Flon Daily Miner — the end of Flin Flon's first newspaper, February 11, 1966. (Reminder)

Flin Flon Hotel on fire, June 9, 1962. (Reminder)

Postal Strike, 1968. (Reminder)

Josiah Flintabbatey Flonatin, June 1962. (Reminder)

Flinty's promotion day, June 29, 1962. (Trout Festival)

Official opening of Bakers' Narrows Lodge, 1965. (Reminder)
(Reminder)

Official opening of the Air Terminal at Bakers' Narrows, November 2, 1968. Left to right: Bill Anderson, Department of Transportation; Gerald Cobb, MP for Portage la Prairie cutting ribbon; Mayor Jack Freedman. (Reminder)

Municipal Airport, 1968. (Reminder)

149

REX RIDEOUT   DAN WARWARUK   DON DONALDSON   DAVE RAINVILLE   BOB WILLEY   GEO. CHIGOL   TOM DAVIE

1965 FLIN FLON WARRIORS 1966
CANADIAN INTERMEDIATE HOCKEY CHAMPIONS

    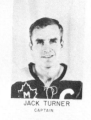 

VIC POIRIER   CLIFF LENNARTZ ASST. CAPT.   GEO. ALLARD MANAGER   EDMONTON JOURNAL TROPHY   JACK TURNER CAPTAIN   KEN KVERN ASST. CAPT.   LAVERN LOEWEN

LYLE WILLEY   RALPH LYNDON   JIM BRYSON TRAINER   BRUCE KEDDIE PRESIDENT   BUD KILLICK COACH   ERNIE POIRIER   HARRY BEUCHERT

BILL BOND   AL WHEELER PUBLICITY   DR. P. PREMACHUK PHYSICIAN   STEVE CARA HON. DIRECTOR   JIM RHEAUME TREASURER   RAY ROGERS ASST. TRAINER   AL EVASON

Flin Flon Midget Bombers Manitoba Provincial Representatives in Centennial Tournament Midget Hockey Championship, 1965-1966. Left to right Back Row: Doug Dutcawich, Garry Westbury, Dale Garinger, Robbie McKenzie, Jules Carrier, Tom Dahl, Ron Allard. Centre Row: Bruce Perkins (Manager), Bob Dickson, Bob Alcorn, Ray Lavitt, Tim Leslie, Gary McKay, Jack Weseen, Roy Jarvis (Coach). Front Row: Kelly Cross, Leigh Allard, Dennis Hyndman, Ray Martiniuk, Blair Costello. Stick Boy — Billy McIntyre. (Roy Jarvis)

Manitoba and Saskatchewan Champions 1967-1968 — Midget Bombers. Left to right Back Row: Gerald Petryk, Blaine Winter, Gord Ferg, Garry Willey, Dave Burr. Centre Row: Roy Jarvis (Coach), Larry Logan, Clarence Pettersen, Don Hollett, Drew Moore, Gord Goodman, Joe Williams, Brian Law, Arnold Kitch (Manager). Front Row: Ron McIntosh, Dale Garinger, Ray Lavitt, Doug Dutcawich, John Laidlaw, Miles St. Godard (Goalie), Stick Boy — Billy McIntyre. (Ron Jarvis)

Western Canada Junior Hockey League Champions 1967-1968. Left to right Back Row: John Roy, Ron Burwash, Murray Anderson, Cal Swenson, Larry Klewchuk, Keith Tomasson. Centre Row: Jake Klewchuk, Nick Oklobdzija (Trainer), Wayne Hawrysh, Lou Morrison, Ron Dundas, Jim Trewin, Brian Marchinko, Terry Dolinsky, Steve Andrascik, Nyall Hyndman (President). Front Row: Craig Reichmuth, Gerry Hart, Chris Worthy, Pat Ginnell (Coach — Manager), Ray Martiniuk, Bob Clarke, Reg Leach, Billy McIntyre (Stick Boy). (Flin Flon Community Club)

151

Glee Club production — Oklahoma, 1960. (J. E. Goodman).

'Out of the Blue' Orchestra performed at Expo 1967. Left to right: Brett Davie, Bill Putko, Murray Trondson, Del Ward, Paul Bergman. (Trout Festival)

Peter McRae and Cathy Price Music Festival winners. (Reminder)

Centennial Dancers, April 1967. Left to right Front Row: Elsie Pearson, Doreen Dunbar, Phyllis and Jim Harburn, Alice Walton, Kathleen Nyuli, Mary McKercher. Second Row: Josie LeClerc, Joyce Armstrong, Mary Grudgfield, Rudy Nyuli, Jackie Gate, Tony Pearson, Ruth Yeo, Norm LeClerc, L ila Kinsley, Mabel McInnes, Mary-Alice Pearson. Third Row: Sid Yeo, Ray Kinsley, Frank Pearson, Doug Armstrong, Cece Walton, Don Grudgfield, Don Gate, Tom McKercher, Reg McInnes, Dave Dunbar. (Trout Festival)

Mayor Freedman and his 'blackboard',
1965-1970. (Reminder)

Earl Watson presented First Aid certificates and scrolls to ten candidates who
successfully completed a course sponsored by the Emergency Measures
Organization, May 6, 1967. Left to right: Earl Watson, Gordon King, Ron
Dodds, Norm Schiltroth, Wayne Wallaker, Dick Evans. Front Row: Maria
Yurkemik, Loretta Yauck, Katherine Matzer, Irene Allen, Beatrice Shirran.
(Reminder)

Tri Service Banquet, May 1967. Left to right: Bob Barr — Kinsmen,
Mickey Perepeluk — Rotary, Con Genik — Rotary, Magistrate Rice —
Guest Speaker, Ed Yauck — Lions Club. (Reminder)

Left to right: Alex Imrie, Jim Conner, Forbes Duncan, Harry
Easton, Gunnar Folkestone, Claude Joyce, John Nikel and
Jack Freedman. (Reminder)

Harry Fenster, Rotary Club, presents new Canadian Flag to
Mayor Jack Freedman, 1966. (Reminder)

Hon. Maitland Steinkopf, chairman of the Manitoba Centennial
Corporation presents Centennial Flag to Sue Anderson, chair-
person of the local Centennial Advisory Committee, June 1966.
(Reminder)

153

Archery Club members, March 1969. (Reminder)

Skeet Club members — Tony Spooner and Pat Ferg, March 1969. (Reminder)

Junior Rifle Club members, 1963. (Reminder)

Junior Rifle Club members, G. Doverspike on the right, June 1968. (Reminder)

Game and Fish Association, 1966. Left to right Back Row: Pat Ferg, N. Lee, Jim Conner, Don Gate, Bill Sweeney, Fred Wilcox. Front Row: Dennis Boen, Fay Switzer, R. Switzer, Elsie Schneider, Jim Robertson. (Junior Rifle Club)

154

Figure Skating Carnival, April 1966 — Animals. (Flin Flon Figure Skating Club)

Susan Trondson and Randy Perepeluk, Senior Mixed Pair — Club Trophy, 1967. (Reminder)

Sue McNeil received the HBM&S Trophy from Earl McDonald, April 1967. (Reminder)

Figure Skating Carnival, April 1966. Left to right: Wendy Frechette, Heather McDougall, Carrie Lynn Frechette, Roberta Fredeen, Sue McNeil, Myrna Chlan. (Flin Flon Figure Skating Club)

Royal Purple, April 1960. Left to right Back Row: Effie Fisher, Hedy Atkinson, Francis Oliver, Gwen Brooks, Bertha Manns, Rita Pettersen, Joanne Gordon, Audrey Reeves, Judy Snell, Eva Jeffrey, Esther Guymer, Hazel Reese. Middle Row: Vera Kepper, Ellen Beilby, Helen Rozek, May Booth, Amber Craig, Lil Akre, Edith Buxton, Irene Brice, Anne Mackonka, Patty Davies, Francis Skwark, Terry Jones, Anna May, Anne Johnsgaard, Ida Pockett, Anna Mack, Edith Smith, Mary Snell, Muriel Burrows. Front Row: Helen McDonald, Helen Roberts, Perle Hume, Ellen Cutt, Marjorie Mason, Edith Anderson, Alma MacDougall. (E. Cutt)

Order of Demolay instituted May 21 and 22, 1966. (Reminder)

International Order of Job's Daughters instituted March 28, 1964. Marilynn Dalgleish was one of the charter members. (Campbell's)

Demolay Flower Talk. Left to right Back Row: George Williams, Monty Woods, Bob Willox, Mitch Njegovan. Centre Row: Chris Dickens, Ken Tokle, Rick Alexander, Gary Walker, Tom Donaghy, Darrell Nowosad, Rod Alexander, Ray Pitt. Front Row: Steven Dzubinski, Bill Lyle, Richard Kerschtein, Fred Howard, Frank·Snorro, Barry Krøller, Ken Dowding, Duncan Walker, Brad Krepps. Sitting: Bert Mann. (Reminder)

Mayor Freedman proclaims Demolay Week, May 1966. Left to right: Russell Slade, Jack Johnson, Bert Mann, David McAree and Milt Laing. (Reminder)

Pine Line Toastmistress Club received Charter June 1966. Left to right: Kay Uhrich, Mrs. Sime, Fern Rudd, Edna Hopkinson, Evelyn Ginsburg and Carol Nicole. (Reminder)

Pinkie Davie and family honored at a farewell party, November 1967. Left to right: Son Brett, Pinkie, Fred Burton, Mrs. Davie and daughter Shelley. (Reminder)

Cairn erected to honor Flin Flon's pioneers, July 1965. (H. Miles)

Club 27 members at the dedication of the Pioneer's Cairn, 1965. (J. Henderson)

THIS CAIRN IS DEDICATED TO THE MEN AND WOMEN WHO WITH GREAT COURAGE CAME NORTH IN THE EARLY DAYS AND CONTRIBUTED SO MUCH TO THE DEVELOPMENT OF THE HUDSON BAY MINING AND SMELTING CO., LIMITED AND LAID THE FOUNDATIONS FOR THIS PROSPEROUS AND HAPPY COMMUNITY.

— o —

THEY BUILDED BETTER THAN THEY KNEW.

ERECTED — A.D. 1965

Plaque on cairn reads: (HBM&S)

Centennial Canoe Team raced from Rocky Mountain House, Alberta to Expo '67 Montreal. Left to right Seated: Norm Crerar, Jim Rheaume, Gib McEachern. Standing: Johnny Norman, Blair Harvey, Joe Michelle, Don Starkell, Roger Carriere, Davey Wells and Wayne Soltys. (Canadian Centennial Commission)

Ted Mackonka with a prize winning 44 pound trout, July 1966. (Reminder)

Trout Festival 'Over 20 Club', 1966. Leone Grayson landed the largest lake trout. (Trout Festival)

Queen Mermaid Luncheon sponsored by the Rotary Club, 1966. (Trout Festival)

Queen Mermaid Ball. (Trout Festival)

Al Warrington cuts ribbon to offically open bonspiel, February 1967. (Reminder)

Ladies' Bonspiel Centennial Style, 1967. Left to right: Jessie Hill, Lil Mitchell, Joy Longmore, Anne Paddock. (Reminder)

Hudson Bay Mining and Smelting Co., Limited winners, 1967. Left to right: Wilf Watt, Ray Quinn, Dick Berthiaume, John Akert. (Reminder)

Opening of the Elks Bonspiel, January 1967. Kelly Stevenson doing the honors. (Reminder)

Winners of Lavitt's Trophy, 1967. Left to right: Millie Mark, Anna Pelletier, Jack Lavitt, Olga Gurba, Ann Galant. (Reminder)

Sir Maurice Roche School Curling, January 1967. Left to right: Rick Gira, Hugh McIntyre, Garry Stewart, Vicke Hayes. (Reminder)

Sod turning for Centennial Building, left to right: Rob Schiefele, Devilyn Dembinsky, Mayor Freedman, George Evans, Sandy Morrice, 1966. (Reminder)

Centennial Library float in Trout Festival Parade. (Reminder)

Official opening of Library, July 1967 — School Children's Choir. (Reminder)

W. A. Green and George Mainwaring broke through the 'rock' to officially open the Centennial building, July 1967. (Trout Festival)

Men's Choir participated in the Centennial Building official opening 1967. (Reminder)

Centennial project for the Parks Board was to place boxes of shrubs and trees on Main Street. Left to right: two Parks Board employees (unknown), H. Whitbread, Russ Jones, Mayor Freedman, Sue Anderson, Norma Tissot, Elmer Thompson and Bud Jobin, May 1967. (Campbell's)

And at the Collegiate. Left to right: G. Grindle, N. Tissot, Mayor Freedman, G. Dougall, Ray Lavitt, G. Craig, J. Nilson, Earl Overland, Betty Klewchuk, May 1967. (Campbell's)

Salvation Army Sunday School children release balloons filled with their names and addresses, January 21, 1967. (Reminder)

R.C.M.P. Musical Ride, 1967. (Reminder)

Friendship Walk 1968 — music to make the time pass. (Reminder)

Dan Popp walked every Friendship Walk. (Reminder)

Chris and Jack Reed on the Friendship Walk 1968. (Reminder)

Eugene Rheaume and grandson John Premachuk take in the Walk, 1968. (Reminder)

Trout Festival Parade, 1968. (Trout Festival)

Beard Growing Contest during the Trout Festival of 1969. (Reminder)

'Up with Us' entertained at one of the 1971 Trout Festival Fish Fries. (Reminder)

Bowlers, February 1967. Left to right: Al Kritzer, Ursula Torrie, Sandy Davie, and Walter Kensick who presented the Westfair Products Trophy, February 1967. (Reminder)

Consolation Five Pin winners, May 1969. Left to right: Lloyd Young, Norma Poirier, Hank Parsons (sponsor), Nell Parsons, Ernie Chocholik (Stag Bowling Lanes), Flo Berry. (Reminder)

Mel's Taxi — winner of the Five Pin Bowling Championship, May 1969. Left to right: Marg Case, Dave Barrett, Lyle Garrioch (sponsor), Marg Barrett, Fred Burton (presented Labatt's trophy), Milly Garrioch, Ken Wright. (Reminder)

Rotary Club Curling Trophy, 1969. Left to right: Harry Fenster, Earl McDonald, Howard McIntosh, Don Stone, Otto Bergman, Alf Boyce. (Reminder)

Harry Bryden Memorial Curling Trophy presented to Erv Hilliard (left), Spud McKenzie, Roy Davidson and Ab Pogue, April 1969. (Reminder)

President's Curling Trophy won by Kay McLaren (left), Norm Rudd, Elaine Wilson and Barry Dickens, April 1969. (Reminder)

Minor Hockey League Executive, 1969. Left to right Back Row: G. George, S. Hughes, L. Brough, L. Benson, J. Boychuk, R. Douglas. Front Row: E. Kelly, F. Phillips, V. Windfield, F. Ledieu. (Reminder)

Flin Flon Junior Bombers were presented with blazers from HBM&S, 1967.

Father Athol Murray presented trophy to Reg Leech of the Bombers, 1969. (Reminder)

BOBBY CLARKE

Bobby Clarke, No. 1 draft choice, 1969. (Y. Clarke)

Chamber of Commerce sponsored 'Winter Wonderland' trip, January 1969. (Reminder)

Mayor Freedman received a special citation for pedestrian safety, October 1969, from Fred Ferguson, while Saul Nathanson looks on. (Reminder)

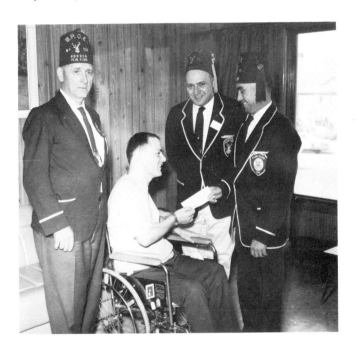

Exalted Ruler B.P.O. Elks J. Jones presented a cheque to Jim Nazar for purchase of Amateur Radio operating equipment. Jim Atkinson (left) and Geoff Mould, July 1969. (Reminder)

Rotary Club entertain at the Senior Citizen's Christmas Party, 1969.

Legion Branch 73 burning their mortgage, September 7, 1971. (Legion)

Thomas Gibney, Hapnot student, represented Canadian Youth at the National Remembrance Day ceremony in Ottawa, November 1972. He received a plaque from Jean Lamy for co-winning the Legion's national literary competition. (Legion)

Kopper Kings represented Zone XI in the Provincial Volleyball Tournament, November 1969. Team members were: Gord Trueman, Bill Vancoughnett, Steve Dzubinski, Rod Hannaford, Fern Brabant, Jamie McIntyre, J. Kurmey (Coach), Rick Willson, Dan McCaig, Blake Willson, Greg Genik, Dennis Nowroski and Doug McGregor. (Hapnot Collegiate)

Cheer Leaders Hapnot Collegiate, 1965. Left to right Standing: Heather Watson, Pat Nielson. Front: Lynn Russell, Bev Shirran, Judy Dembinsky and Myrna Chlan. (E. Robinson)

Flin Flon School Band 1973. (Trout Festival)

Athletes of the Year awards to Dan McCaig and Janet Sparling were presented by principal Gerry Dougall, June 1971. (Reminder)

Knights of Columbus hosted Indoor Games. Left to right Back Row: Jim Brown, Mark Ekstrom, Bob van Nes, David Sheppard, Bill Slugoski, Arthur O'Donnell, Vern Mohr. Centre Row: Joanne Kostiuk, Wendy Taylor, Ellen McAree, Sandy Ferguson, Sue Taylor. Front Row: Bunny Hart, Debbie Jeffries, Michelle Dion, Jim Beilby. (Reminder)

Linda Hutch (left) and Paul Pohlod (right) were first and third winners in the Manitoba Chamber of Commerce sponsored photograph contest. Hugh Bebbington presented the certificates on behalf of the Chamber. Glen Campbell was local organizer. December 1969. (Reminder)

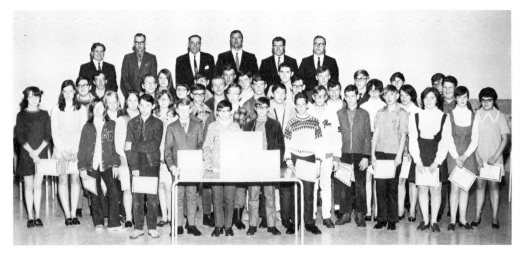

Survival Course graduates with Wildlife Association Instructors, left to right Back Row: Tony Pearson, George Frame, Harry Guymer, Bill Bevans, Tony Spooner and Bill Burbidge, 1970. (HBM&S)

Debbie Ramsay winner of Eaton competition, 1970. (Reminder)

Junior Rifle Hunter and Firearm Safety class with instructors Andy Galambos and George Ramsay (left), Stan Goulden (right), 1970. (Reminder)

Second place winner was Gloria Biletski, 1970. (Reminder)

Game and Fish Trophy held by Harold Bowman, was won by the Junior Rifle Tuesday Night Class. Instructor was Nick Ostash (left), 1970. (Reminder)

Linda Kozar placed third in the Eaton Competition for which she received a rifle from Gerry Fladager of Eaton's, 1970. (Reminder)

Creighton Bantam A's received C. G. Bowles trophy, October 1969. (Reminder)

Birchview Midgets won the Richmond Hotel trophy, October 1969. (Reminder)

Manitoba paddling team, Champions of the British Columbia Centennial Canoe Pageant: John Rutley, Laddie Ballantyne, Marcel Mercredie, Don Starkell, Jim Killick, Ed Erlendson and Gerry Hart, August 1971. (J. Killick)

Kart Derby, 1971. (Reminder)

Sheila Hanson (left), Pat and Joan Conner sang at the Manitoba Concert Hall in the spring of 1972. (Reminder)

Kinsmen School, 1970. (D. Linden)

Mrs. Kearns Class at the Kinsmen School. (Reminder)

Official opening of the Occupational Centre with Buck Witney cutting ribbon, Dot Linden (right), September 19, 1970. (Reminder)

Occupational Centre, 1970. (D. Linden)

Blessed Virgin Mary's Ukrainian Catholic Church. (St. Mary's)

St. Andrew's Presbyterian Church. (St. Andrew's)

Clinic Staff 1950's. Left to right Back Row: Gord Martin, Dr. C. A. Milanese, Dr. P. Johnson, Dr. N. Stephansson, Dr. E. Redpath, Fred Grey, Dr. A. A. Campbell, Dr. H. L. McNichol, W. Andrews, Grace Wiginton. Front Row: Jessie Shepard, Dorothy Low, Madge Glover, Silvia Pangrass, Norma Bell, Addie Plummer, Dorothy Adams, Connie Hammel, Emile Bogash, Josie Donaldson. (Dorothy Low)

Opening of the General Hospital 1951, HBM&S donated the laundry equipment. Sister Remillard and M.A. Roche (centre), Sister Marie on right. (Reminder)

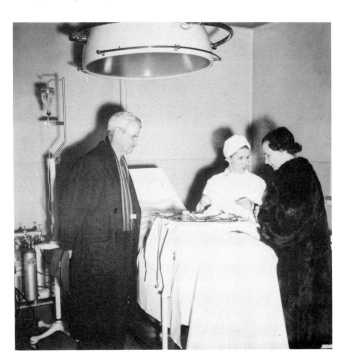

Demonstration in the operating room by Nurse Tester for Mr. and Mrs. Bob Dadson, 1951. (Reminder)

Congratulations to Sister Larocque from Hon. Ivan Schultz, Minister of Health, January 28, 1952. (Reminder)

Left to right: Laura Williamson, Imrie; Margaret Coad, Ross; Lucille (Charlie) Charlebois, Jarvis; Miss Scrapek, 1949. (L. Jarvis)

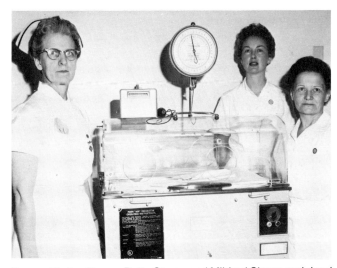

Nurses Marion Kenny, Betty Storey and Mildred Simes explained the new equipment during the opening of the hospital wing, October 1959. (Reminder)

Nurses Association furnished a room in the proposed hospital extension. Mrs. Alice West made the presentation, December 1967. (Reminder)

Ladies of the Royal Purple donated a humidifier for the Pediatric Ward, November, 1968. Left to right: Hedy Atkinson, Sister Superior Mandeville, Betty Storey, Pearl Hankin and Edna Jeffery. (Reminder)

North Star Rebekah Lodge No. 31 made a donation to the pediatric ward, 1978. Left to right: Marie Lewis, Roy Brown, M. Parreno, Jean Hopkins. (Flin Flon General Hospital)

Orange Lodge presented wheelchairs to General Hospital, 1969. Left to right: R. McComb, Sister Guyot, L. Bloxom, Sister Superior, Andy Maxwell, Ann Switzer, Wes Smith and Dorothy Hunter. (Reminder)

Odd Fellows Lodge No. 57 presented a cheque to the General Hospital, 1971. Left to right: Garnet Forsythe, R. McComb, Keith Taylor and Dr. Norm Stephansson. (B. Stephansson)

Canadian Armed Forces Wives Association presented a cheque to the General Hospital, January 1970. Left to right Seated: Mrs. George McLean, Sister Guyot, Mrs. Donald MacDonald. Standing: Mesdames E. Brown, B. Reles, Miss Betty Storey, Mesdames F. Sanford, A. Gauthier and A. West. (Reminder)

Mayor Alex Clark, Creighton and Mayor Jack Freedman, Flin Flon, at the controls of the bulldozer moving rocks and dirt to make way for the new hospital, April 24, 1970. (Reminder)

West side of the General Hospital, 1974. (Val Hedman)

South side of the General, 1974. (Val Hedman)

Official opening of addition to General Hospital, Rene Toupin, Minister of Health and Social Services cuts ribbon, Hospital Board Chairman C. K. Taylor (right). In background left to right: Mayor Alex Clark (Creighton) Carl Edmonds, Andy Stewart and Dave Robertson. (General Hospital)

Dr. Percy Johnson was honored during the month of August 1973. Left to right: Dr. Johnson, Bud Jobin, Dr. Harvey McNichol and Mrs. McNichol. (HBM&S)

The City of Flin Flon presented an ambulance to the General Hospital. Left to right: Denny Beaudin, Isabel Stewart, Dr. N. Stephansson, Mayor Howard Abrahamson (1978), Ken Shoemaker, Earl Watson. (Reminder)

Company Hospital closed its doors in February 1972. (HBM&S)

Company Hospital personnel, 1972. Left to right: Myrna Graham, Irene Young, Leone Govenlock, Hazel Nisbet, Peggy McCormick, Ethel Killick, Ruth Ekstrom and Elaine Duffy. (Hazel Nisbet)

Left to right: Mike (Health Board Chairman) and Edie Chlan, Dr. and Betty Johnson, Jim and Shirley Goodman, December 1971. (Hazel Nisbet)

Nurses at the Clinic 1973. Left to right: Marg Vance, Joan Edwards, Sally Bauman, Donni Jobin. (S. Jarvis)

Bernadette 'Dettie' Reles. (Hap Reles)

Company Hospital staff 1970. Left to right: Anna McDonald, Betty McGregor, Hazel Nisbet, Elene Blake, Bernice Jones, Mary Gokey, Alice Olson. (H. Nisbet)

Company Hospital staff 1971. Left to right: Carol Banick, Leone Govenlock, Hazel Nisbet, Myra Stonehouse. (H. Nisbet)

Garden party at Bakers' Narrows 1971. Left to right Back Row: Gerns Sparling, Evelyn Pearson, Phil Simpson, Eileen Munro, Arlene Sorenson, Ella Hughes. Centre: Peggy Barker, Katherine Miles, Shirley Shnider. Front: Eleanor Sparling, Elizabeth Johnson, Vivian Reed, Eva Fairburn and Mrs. Gus Brownrigg. (B. Stephansson)

Edra Johnson retired as Senior Public Health Nurse in 1972. (E. Johnson)

Norm 'Red' Bernard retired in October 1975 and received a farewell gift from Dale Powell, Industrial Relations. Red operated the Blood Donor Clinic in Flin Flon for 26 years. (Bruce Reid)

Opening of hospital, 1971, some of the original nurses who worked in the old hospital. Left to right: Lucille Jarvis (Charlebois), Kay Burr (Wagner), Sister Maseau and Laura Imrie (Williamson). (Flin Flon Hospital)

Clinic Staff — left to right Standing: Ruby Evans, Emilie Hillier, Chris Alexander, Rena Poirier. Seated: Babe Willis and Dorothy Low. (Rena Poirier)

Sisters who were teachers at Sir Maurice Roche School. Left to right Back Row: Sisters Josephat, Kelly, Phillip and Eleanor. Front Row: Sisters Clair Jobin, Irene Lucille and Audrey. (B. Stephansson)

Members of the Catholic Women's League who received 25 year pins and scrolls, May 1970. Left to right: Jean Hook, Elizabeth Krassilowsky, Evelyn Pearson, Cecilia Huber, Katherine Matzer, Father Nolan, Charlotte Willey, Anna Sikler, Mary Fieber, Stella Rheaume and Pat Schiefele. (K. Matzer)

Fire at the Manor housing project, 1971. (Reminder)

Northern Lights Manor looking west, 1972. (David Price)

Official opening of Northern Lights Manor, February 1972. Left to right: Mayor Ed Yauck (1971-1974), Loretta Yauck, Lily Schreyer and Premier Ed Schreyer. (J. Henderson)

Tea at the Manor with Ann Hudak pouring, February 1973. Left to right: Carrie Seaman, Ruth McIntosh, Mabel Sproxton, Olga Dumenko, Myrtle Quesnell and Buck Hay. (Manor)

Ten year employees at Northern Lights Manor, 1982. Left to right: Lena Kopachinski, Alice Grudgfield, Ethel Thompson, Pauline Woloshyn, Olga Dumenko. (Manor)

Tenth Anniversary Tea, June 1982. Left to right Back Row: Phyllis Antal, Mrs. Jackson, Betty Edworthy, Pat Kawerski, Irene Stein, Pauline Woloshyn, Bernie LaCroix, Melba Mayner. Middle: Charlotte Nickel, Alice Grudgfield, Sarah Roy, Gail Nowrocki, Jane Hedman, Bette Williams, Hazel Highfield. Front: Lena Kopachinski, Ethel Thompson, Olga Dumenko, Sheila Adams, Lorna Mayner and Alex Roncin. (Manor)

Composite staff of Rebekahs travelled to Winnipeg, March 1972. Left to right Back Row: Edie Chlan, Lillian Wilson, Verna Goodwin, Gail Martin, Ev Pico, Mae Greenberg, Ann Chell. Middle Row: Pat Vatcher, Mary Brown, Arlene Souter, Jackie Gate, Janet McAree, Grace Burgess, Ericka Stenbeck. Front Row: Esther Guymer, Betty McGregor, Marie Lewis, Greta McEachern (President of the Manitoba Rebekah Assembly), Doreen Willson, Joyce Henderson, Irene Lowes. (J. Henderson)

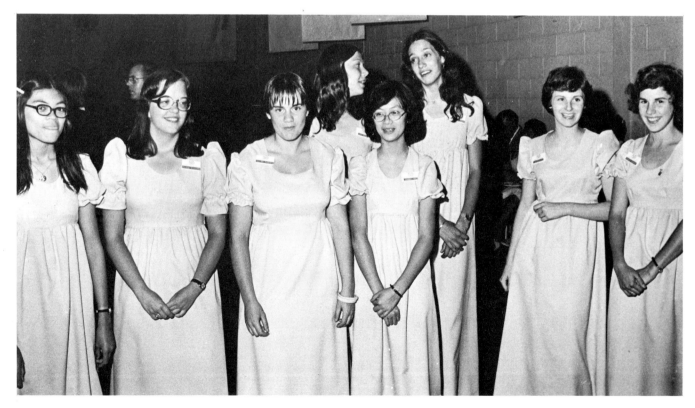

Flinkore Theta Rho Girls' Club No. 5 (instituted August 1975) ushered at HBM&S 50th Anniversary at the Community Hall, July 1977. Left to right: Nancy Yee, Arlene Willson, Louise Roberts, Bev Dash, Donna Yee, Monique Popp, Lisa Garuk and Cathy James. (HBM&S)

Topping off the 825 foot stack on Company property — July 1973. (HBM&S)

1972-1973 Midget Bombers (Bantam A winners of Tribune Trophy) Left to right Front Row: Ron Henry (Trainer), Derek Rideout, Bob Dougall, Bill Maluta (Coach), Tom Snyder, Kelly Petalik, Richie Budlong (Ass't Coach). Middle Row: Murray Davidson (President), Kevin Rogers, Rolly Rice, Ron Barr, Bruce Gibson, Pat Woods, Hugh Devlin, Fraser Dougall, Kim Anderson. Back Row: Ricky Chlan, Garry Fischer, Ron Reader, Lyle Mitchell, Brant McCombie, Kevin Brothers and Terry Davis. (Reminder)

Manitoba Midget AA Champions 1974. Left to right Back Row: Murray Davidson (President of Minor Hockey League), Roy Jarvis (Coach), Eddie Hagan, Tom Cullen, Joey Rowlett, Les Bray, Pete McCombie, Darell Graff, Bruce Gibson, Fraser Dougall, Kim Davis, Charlie Cook, Derek Rideout, Kevin Brothers, Arnold Kitch (Manager). Front: Bob Dougall, Hughie Devlin, Don Henry, Brent Kristoff, Ron Reader, Kelly Petalik, Cal Enright. (R. Jarvis)

Conservation Officer's home in Channing, 1975. (Bruce Reid)

Conservation Officer Mike Kotyk and Frank Guymer, 1975. (F. Guymer)

Building bird enclosures at Willowvale Animal Park, 1975. (Reminder)

Guy Henderson (left) and Scott Fladager, members of the Young Trappers' Association, 1978. (Glen Henderson)

Award of Merit presented to Mr. and Mrs. Gordon Roberts by Bob Davison on behalf of the Horticulture Society, 1972. (Gordon Grindle)

Mrs. D. Willis receives Award of Merit from Bob Davison, 1973. (G. H. Grindle)

Bal Dor Trophy — Grand Aggregate — presented to Gordon Grindle by Bob Davison, 1970. (Gordon Grindle)

Life membership in the Horticulture Society was presented to Bal Biggs by John Wilson and Gordon Grindle. (G. H. Grindle)

Flin Flon Horticulture Society. Left to Right: Bob Davison, Tom Willey, Mavis Burwash, Gren Scott, Ruth Roncin, Les Saville, Sue Perepeluk, Charlotte Willey, Ada Russell, Marg Rumbal, Margaret Wingert, Alex Roncin, Thor Pockett. (G. H. Grindle)

Canada Cords were presented at the Legislative Building to (left to right) Kathy Kolebaba (The Pas), Valerie Henderson, Lila Kubat and Theresa Folwark. Ruth Bunn, Cambrian Area Commissioner, accompanied the Girl Guides, March 25, 1972. (Mathews Photo Studio)

Kevin Weber presented with certificate of Meritorious Conduct by Ralph Heard, Regional Scout Executive of Manitoba Western Region, November 1971. (Reminder)

Jeffrey Gordon and Kevin Weber rescued Marty Burton from Flin Flon Creek, November 1971. (Reminder)

Casmeara Clark received the Bronze Stage of the Duke of Edinburgh Award in Guiding from Mayor Nazir Ahmad, 1982. (C. Thomas)

4H group of gardeners, 1981. (G. H. Grindle)

World War I Veterans were honored at Canadian Legion's 50th Anniversary 1975. Left to right Front Row: Axel Christianson, Tom Lyons, Arnie Akert, Gislie Norman, Russ Blackman, Fred Lloyd, Dave Morre, W. Medd. Back Row: Stan Cox (Legion President), Percy Carriage, Jake Johnson, Frank Vanderbush, Jack Johnson, Jim Aplin, Dave Lahonen, Ron Highfield. (Provincial Command) (Bruce Reid)

Legion Pipe Band, 1975. Left to right Front Row: Rob Killick, Greg Anderson, Janice LaRocque, Carla Craig, Kim Wilson, Allison Mitchell, Pat Lengyel, Grace MacDonald. Middle: Nancy Snider, Margaret Hanna, Gordon Stevens, Naomi Dalgleish, Vicky Dojcak, Jane Craig, Tracy Pruder, John Ringrose, Kathy Wilson, Wendy Radchuck. Back Row: Chris Anderson, Graham Craig, David Hanna, Jim Fell and Kent Pollard. (Bruce Reid)

Barber Shop Polecats, 1976. Left to right: Ron Price, Earl Watson, Jim Goodman, Harold Vance. (Bruce Reid)

HBM&S 50th anniversary — All Male Choir conducted by Jim Goodman, performed at Phantom Lake, July 1, 1977. (Bruce Reid)

Generation Gap at Sportsnight '76, Trout Festival. (Bruce Reid)

1977 Trout Festival Queen Eldene Mohr. (Trout Festival)

Gold Rush Canoe Race 1977. (Trout Festival)

Trout Festival Bed Race 1977. (Trout Festival)

Flour packing at the Trout Festival — Beaver Lake Day 1977. (Trout Festival)

Pancake Breakfast at the Festival 1977. Left to right: Doug O'Brien, Steve Kowalewich, Harry Yee and Ralph Klimack. (Trout Festival)

Lieutenant Governor, Lawrence F. (Bud) Jobin and Donni at Government House, 1977. (B. Stephansson)

Mayor Bruce Keddie (April to December 1977) (HBM&S)

Flin Flon pioneers received Honorary Citizens' Award from the City, July 1977. Some receiving this award were: The Eilert Hagan family, Angus Ross, Margaret Germain, Leona Grayson, Frank and Bertha Gummerson, Harry and Esther Guymer, Sid Hudson, Dave and Irene McGilvray, Algot and Viola Mosell, Harry and Inez Ennis, Ralph and Louise Bloomfield. (HBM&S)

Welcome Home Party at Beaver Lake, July 1977, for Club '27 members and other early pioneers. Left to right Back Row: Ralph Bloomfield, George Winterton, Dave McGilvray, Harry Ennis, Ed Hagan, Harry Guymer, Bertha and Frank Gummerson, Jim and Ole Hagan. Middle Row: Glen Rapson, Angus Ross, Leona Grayson, Inez Ennis, Esther Guymer, unkown, Peg Rapson, Connie Hagan. Front Row: Arnie Akert, Irene McGilvray, Ivy Hagan, William Dodds, Lila Stevens, Margaret Germain. (HBM&S)

Arlene Sorenson and Ruth Shomperlen during a display of local art work. (Bruce Reid)

Joe and Sophie Jakubcak at Folklorama, May 1977. (Bruce Reid)

Display from Holland. Left to right: Hendrica Akkerman, Elly Trudeau, Jan and Eef Akkerman, 1976. (E. Trudeau)

Ukrainian display booth with Pearl Mendro (left), Rose Maluta and Mary Skwarchuk, 1977. (Reminder)

The Bridge Club travelled to Waskisew to compete 1977. Left to right Back Row: John Munson, John Ross, Brian Wallace, Bob Murray. Middle Row: Geri Kostuchuk, Bernice Joyner, Wayne Black, Irene Ross, Irene Fenwick, Marge Woloshyn, Ed Gauthier. Front Row: Jean Runehjelm, Kay Uhrich, Evelyn Black, Elaine Murray, Cay Jorundson, Rena Coulter and Bessie Eryou. (HBM&S)

Jim Goodman (right) offers congratulations to Harry Miles who retired after nine years as editor of the Northern Lights, December 1975. (Bruce Reid)

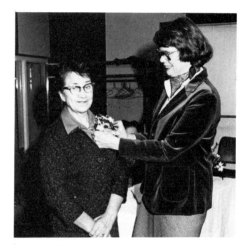

Irene Hutton (left) was honored at an 'Irene Hutton Night', 1981. Neta deVette pins on her corsage. (HBM&S)

Mayor Howard Abrahamson and his Council 1978-1979. Left to right Back Row: Howard Pascoe, Nazir Ahmand, Charles Whitbread, Peter Mendro. Front Row: John Rutley, Mayor Abrahamson, Gunnar Folkestone. (Bruce Reid)

Flin Flon Aqua Centre opened June 28, 1975. (Reminder)

Ed Yauck and Sue Taylor at the opening of the Aqua Centre, June 28, 1975. (Reminder)

Norman Games at the Aqua Centre, 1975. (HBM&S)

Synchronized Swimmers, April 1983. Left to right Back Row: Lynne Hagberg (Coach), Marla Fieber, Corrie Harris, Tiffany Hagberg, Paige Cardell, Nicole Menzies, Tara Black, Maureen Pogue (Coach). Middle Row: Kari Nisbet, Natasha Tkach, Angie Wood, Karen Nagy, Diane Ledoux, Pam Hogarth. Back Row: Dustin Smith, Melani Hyska, Tanya Kozar, Wendy Stewart. (Bruce Keddie)

Aqua Jets, March 10, 1983. Left to right, Back Row: Linda Kozar, Ken Slater, Sherrie Husberg, Wade Langin, Casmeara Clark, Melissa Skwarchuk, Leonard Skwarchuk. Fourth Row: Cameron Bottrell, Samantha Thomas, Hillary Mills, Robin Hill, Tracy Fraik, Shauna Donaldson, Tamara Allen. Third Row: Jason Mills, Stephanie Kurmey, Lori Langin, Susan Fell, Jenny Crozier, Trena Allan. Second Row: Gillian Weseen, Carmen Hiebert, Carmen Weseen, Sandy Zolinski, Laura Lee Brown, Wanda Olson. Front Row: Trevor Miller, Jason Langin, Jenny Jarvis, Heather Burgess, Wendy Morrison. (Reminder)

Hanger #16, December 1978. Left to right Back Row: Sgt. Harry Sentner, Anderson, Lee Cook, Monica Herman, Cheryl Stasko, Marie Chretian, Skip Martin (Bus Driver), Michael Knopff, Mrs. Beauchamp, Ed Wilson, Sandy Cooper, Lt. Lahonen, Val Meachem, Valeta Hogarth, Bob Saul, Darcy Miller, Gilroy, Joycelyn Duazo, Grant Schubert, Danny Meachem, Kirk Abrahamson, Guide. Front Row: Keith Saul, George Conway, Rachelle Rainville, Jim Keddie, Norman Winter, Ron Quaal, Stephen Prieur, Loreen Herriot, Rick Quaal, John Balfour, Ian Saul, Dwayne Hanson, Wayne Cooper, Reg Quaal, Billy Kostuchuk, Ward Einarson. (Armouries)

21st Field Squadron 1977. Left to right Back Row: Dave Sigurdson, Bob Penner, Orville Roncin, Eric Kerfont, Spr. Derkatch, Vernon Kaus, Clarence Kitson, Brenda Danko, Bart Kohlmeyer, Fred Baker, Bev Zollen, Wayne Harkin, Spr. Bouteillier. Middle Row: Barry Dickens, Henry Chaisson, Bill Bernhard, Mike Kohlmeyer, Bob Donogh, Doug Gourlay, Larry Salvail, Grant Aune, Tony Haffick, Gordon Bryson, Ron Ballantyne, Dale Coble, Mike Kish, Don Zollen, Fred Baxter. Front Row: Bud Horrocks, Bob Maguire, Dan Gunn, Fred Baker, Frank Gira, Morley Naylor, Dennis Rivet, Ed Martel, George Danko, Mike Kryschuk. (Bruce Reid)

Authors of the Flin Flon History Book published February 1974. Left to right: Loretta Yauck, Val Hedman and Joyce Henderson. (J. Henderson)

Betty Carpen author of Hardship and Happiness, 1976. (Reminder)

Trail of the Wild Goose written by Hank Parsons, 1978. (Bruce Reid)

Best in Manitoba, Tom Thumb Champions, TMCC Bombers 1978-1979. Left to right Front Row: Kevin Garinger, Donnie Hynes, Jimmy Collins, Kevin Huculiak, Mark Kritzer, Dean Owen, Mel Merasty, Todd Clark, Mike Thorley. Middle Row: Chris Nisbet, Trent Hill, Robbie LaValley, Chris Weseen, Darwin McPherson, Lee Ayling, Dwayne Warga, Mike Linnick, Kenny Garinger. Back Row: Roger Poirier (Coach), Steve Takacs (TMCC), Terry Brown (Manager), Ken Stenicki (Ass't Coach). (Rena Poirier)

Scorpio Bantam Bombers, Manitoba Champions, 1983. Left to right Back Row: Mike Thorley, Reid Simpson, Don Hynes, Michael Linnick, Mark Kritzer. Middle Row: Darrell Johnson, Darwin McPherson, Chris Weseen, Rob LaValley, Tim Madarash, Lee Ayling, Duane Warga. Front Row: Aaron Chigol, Dan Diakow (Ass't Coach), Dean Owen, Glen LaValley (Manager), Sheldon Sendecki, Brad Snyder (Coach), Chris Nisbet. (Reminder)

RCMP and Fire Hall Complex opened January 27, 1981. (Reminder)

Fire Hall, men and equipment, 1982. (Jubilee Committee)

Old Fire Hall, 1981. (Fire Department)

Lieutenant Governor F. L. Jobin and Mayor Nazir Ahmad cut the ribbon with fire axes to officially open the new RCMP-Fire Hall Complex, January 27, 1981. (Fire Department)

Firemen 1980. Left to right Front Row: Mike Trubiak, Earl Steven, Cliff Clarke, Reuben Hagan, Dan Still, Jim Finucane, Lawrence Moran, Charlie Jones. Second Row: Joe Wilson, Ehart Dzuibak, Don Logan, Tom Davie, Vic Pardowski, Dave Broughton, Barry Dickens, Don Rose, Larry Willerton, Bill Reed. Third Row: Brain McLaren, Randy McLaren, Wes Mote, Rick Switzer, Jamie Pitelburg, Hugh Devlin, Gordon Donaghy, Calvin Ballard, Norm Rudd. (Jubilee Committee)

Flin Flon clinic opened in July, 1982. (Scott Burke)

Bud and Donni Jobin officially cut the ribbon to open the Clinic, July 1982. (S. Shnider)

Doctors in the Clinic 1982. Left to right: S. M. Amin, R. Bailey, A. Esmail, W. J. Donaldson, M. Shnider and K. Sethi. (S. Shnider)

Evergreen Rebekah Lodge No. 56 donated two lounge chairs to the Northern Lights Manor, January 1983. Left to right: Mary Billy, Marilyn Ridley (PNG of Evergreen), Charlotte Nickel (Manor Co-ordinator), Flora Warren (NG of Evergreen) and Lou McArthur. (Reminder)

Dave and Mabel Watt and Emery Switzer, just some of the residents of Hemlock Drive Elderly Persons Housing Complex, January 1983. (Reminder)

Circle C, St. James Anglican Church, and guests, January 1982. Left to right Back Row: Jackie Gate, Sandy, Bertha and Joyce Gummerson, Ann Warrington, Queenie Williamson, Marg Sebescen, Joyce Henderson, June McFadden. Centre Row: Ethel Killick, Ann Davison, Evelyn Zimmerman, Ev Pico. Front Row: Nell Cutt, Helen McKenzie, Jean Hopkins, Hazel Nisbet, Ann Beveridge and Eileen Munro. (H. Nisbet)

Tri Service Ladies, 1981-1982. Left to right: Helen Heinz (Lion L's), Judy Kissick (Kinettes), Diana Diggle (Lion L's) and Marion Davidson (Rotary Anns). (Lion L's)

Royal Bank celebrates 50 years, 1982. Left to right: Marilyn Bergman, Bev Goodfellow, Sophie Riehl, Yvonne Harvie. (Royal Bank)

Bryan Minnis (left) and Dave Hider, Royal Bank 50th, 1982. (Royal Bank)

Prayer Breakfast, 1982. Left to right: Mayor Nazir Ahmad, Premier Howard Paulley, Keith Callander (General Manager HBM&S), Lieutenant Governor Pearl McGonigal and Gordon Mitchell (Chairman). (N. Ahmad)

Knights of Columbus, 1982-1983. Left to right Back Row: E. Olson, E. Scheiber, R. Greensides, P. Chaisson, J. Vielgut, H. Zahajko, W. Kelly, J. Fernandes. Front Row: N. LeClerc, T. Carmichael, D. Osika, Father Ed Kosa, D. Colli, R. Schiefele, T. Duazo, B. Quinn. (Knights of Columbus)

Pee Wee Baseball 'A' Champions — Angels, 1982. Left to right: Harland Garinger (Coach), Kevin Garinger, Ken Garinger, Robert LaValley, Ken Wynnychenko, Kevin Huculiak, Mark Kritzer, Sheldon Koczka, Blaine Gogal, Tim Madarash, Duane Warga, Mike Thorley, Dean Owen, Tom Mager (Ass't Coach). (Fran Garinger)

Members of the Dart Club represented Northern Manitoba in the Provincial finals, March 27, 1983. Left to right Back Row: Dave Miller, Laurie Balfour, Ray Boudreau, Jack Rigby, Peter Davies, Brian Humphreys, Dave Edwards. Front Row: Brian Hartray, Pam Thomas, Sharon Rigby, Maureen Jackson, Helen Humphreys, Perry Burton. (Reminder)

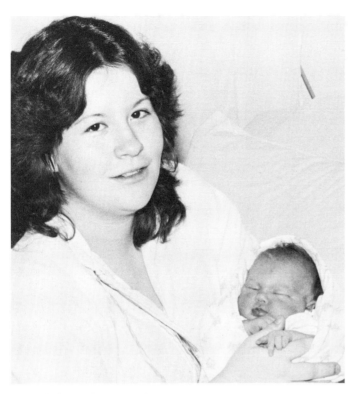

Amanda Dawn Fox, born January 4, 1983, Flin Flon's Jubilee New Year baby and her mother Dawn. (Bruce Keddie)

Jubilee Year got off to a great start with bonfires on January 1, 1983. (S. Jarvis)

And weiners to cook on the bonfires. (S. Jarvis)

Mayor Ahmad presented a complimentary Jubilee Commemorative Silver Coin to Annette Kirby the artist responsible for the design on the coin, March 11, 1983. (Reminder)

Lieutenant Governor Pearl McGonigal was presented with native gauntlets by Del Baird, Chairperson of the Jubilee Committee. Also present were Mayor Ahmad and wife Pat, and Mr. McGonigal, February, 1983. (Jubilee Committee)

Photo 54, 1982. Left to right Front: Bruce Reid, Harry Hobbs, David Johnston, Len Reynolds, Del Brown, Gordon Linnick. Back Row: Mel Schiltroth, Anne Schiltroth, Steven Taylor, Glen Campbell. (Bruce Reid)

Library Staff and Lieutenant Governor Pearl McGonigal, February 1983. Left to right: Blanche Fisher, Kay Matzer, Pearl McGonigal, Dorothy Bridges, Rhonda McKinnon, Trudy Klause, Phyllis Stadnick. (Library)

Shell Cup Competitions Timing Chalet, 1982. (Bernie Lynn)

Ski Club House, 1982. (Jubilee Committee)

Left to right: Ivor Hedman (sponsor of the annual Centaloppet), Tony Spooner and Bill Friesen, 1971. (Val Hedman)

Life members of the Ski Club — Mary Crerar and Art Lyons, 1971. (Val Hedman)

Scott Clark winner of the 1983 Centaloppet Cup. (Reminder)

8th Annual Centaloppet — Jubilee Edition — had 110 cross country skiers participating, February 1983. (Reminder)

Birch bark biting requires fresh birch bark. (Reminder)

Lieutenant Governor Pearl McGonigal watches Angelique Merasty demonstrate birch bark biting, February 1983. (Gloria Taylor)

Angelique Merasty shows Lieutenant Governor McGonigal how her teeth have worn from biting birch bark, while Mr. Merasty watches, February 1983. (Jubilee Committee)

Ladies' Choir practicing for the Lieutenant Governor's visit, February 1983. (Jubilee Committee)

Ukrainian Dancers during the Lieutenant Governor's visit, February 1983. (Jubilee Committee)

Winners of the HBM&S event and the Grand Aggregate during the Ladies' Bonspiel, March 1983. Left to right: Keith Callander (HBM&S General Manager), Dayle Rusk (skip), Denyse Clace, Janet Gourlay, Patrice Ellingson. (Reminder)

Winners of HBM&S and Grand Aggregate in the annual Men's Bonspiel, March 1983. Left to right: Keith Callander (General Manager HBM&S), Glen Benson (skip), Morley Pedwell, John Faktor, Mike Booker. (Reminder)

RCMP Staff Sgt. R. C. Paul presented a cheque to Minor Hockey League President Rene Gregory. The money was raised from the proceeds of a broomball game between the local RCMP Detachment and the Winnipeg Blue Bombers, February 1983. (Reminder)

Curling veterans, January 1983. Left to right: Henry Budlong, Pete Hume, Al Maloney, Rod Chell, Glen Smith. (Reminder)

Figure Skating Club members who competed in Stonewall in February, 1983. Left to right: Gillian Bottrell, Joanne Henry, Scott Brown, Dodie Willis, Lana Kelbert. (Reminder)

Local Figure Skaters, 1981. Left to right Back Row: Cory Gira, Lisa Souter, Kathy Hagan, Dianne Beck. Front Row: Gillian Bottrell, Kim Norman, Carl Stoltz, Allison Martinot. (HBM&S)

Power Skating Champions, February 1983. Left to right: Ashley LaValley, Tyler Brown, Neil Willan, Bryon Lofgren, Craig Beck, Allan Richard. (Reminder)

Bowlers who competed in Thompson in February 1983. Left to right: Peter Pierangeli, Gerry Grindle, Gordie Brown, Doreen Asmus. (Reminder)

Students who were winners in the Knights of Columbus Basketball Free Throw Competition 1983. Left to right: Abigail Dorion, Dawn Angell, Graham Garrett, Vicki Watt. (Reminder)

Slogan winners wear their T-shirts in the Dialogue on Drinking Contest March 1983. Left to right Back Row: Eric Johnson, Ken Shaw, Vicky LeBlanc. Middle Row: Lori Lynne Coles, Tammy Gudbranson, Teri Lynn Odut. Front Row: Dion Knol, Jon Evans, Nancy Paton. (Reminder)

Ruth Betts Junior High School Science Fair winners, April 1983. Left to right: Ronna Finnie, Peter Donahue, Tracy Prysliak. (Reminder)

Flin Flon Lodge #57, I.O.O.F. April, 1983. Back Row, left to right: Keith McCullough, Grant Adams, Bob Ruckle. Middle Row: Mike Chlan, Lawrence Halldorson, John McAree, Bill McArthur, Stewart Evans, Cal Berry, Glen Mikkelsen, Don Bray, Joe Dumenko, Doug Reid, Wray Henderson, Ray Kinsley, Ivan Boyce, Bill Serdinski. Front Row: Len Harris, Garnet Forsythe, Lawrence Brough, Tom Warren, Ted Vancoughnett, Ron Dodds, Peter Fint, George Rideout, Cam Yeo, Lyle Benson, Gord Hayes, Menno Fehr.   (Bruce Reid)

North Star Rebekah Lodge #31, April 1983. Back Row, left to right: Janet McAree, Karen Chaisson, Ruth Shomperlen, Elly Trudeau, Hazel Nisbet, Elizabeth Murray, Marian Dodds, Lauraine Vancoughnett, Emma Knudson, Grace Burgess, Edie Chlan. Front Row: Marian Fraser, Hazel Ellingson, Ethel Thompson, Elsie Thurston, Joyce Henderson, Madalean Stevens, Esther Guymer, Ev Pico, Tammy Lyons, Millie Fint, Judy Beauchamp.   (Bruce Reid)

Evergreen Rebekah Lodge #56, April, 1983. Back Row, left to right: Doug Reid, Tom Warren, Cal Berry, Joe Dumenko, Grant Adams, Menno Fehr. Middle Row: Gladys Neufeld, Annette Mikkelsen, Marg Highmoor, Eleaner Hayes, Olga Dumenko, Betty Maranchuk, Norma Poirier, Bernadette Benson, Lila Hatley, Shirley Davidson, Matilda Mitchell. Front Row: Amy Ruckle, Eleaner Dubeski, Polly Woloshyn, Flora Warren, Hazel Reid, Sheila Adams, Flo Berry, Betty Fehr, Eleanor Boyce, Gaye Bray.   (Bruce Reid)

Flinkore Theta Rho Girls Club #5, April 1983. Back Row, left to right: Kirsten Donaldson, Noreen Shepherd, Shirley Neault, Marilyn Alcorn, Amy Ruckle, Teresa Cap, Shirley Ruckle, Brenda McAree, Gail Boiteau. Front Row: Tammy Lyons, Linda Neault, Nicole Jarvis, Mary-Jo Friesen, Marla Krassilowsky, Susan Burbidge, Laurel Harkin, Stacey Bailey, Judy Beauchamp.   (Bruce Reid)

Flin Flon City Council 1982-1983. Left to right: Peter Mendro, Dick Lyons, Ed VanDoorn, Mayor Nazir Ahmad, Shirley Boyce, Howard Pascoe and Elmer Gohl. (City of Flin Flon)

Greg Bauman was elected in October 1982 to replace Ed Van Doorn on City Council. (Jubilee Committee)

Earl Watson was honored on retirement after fifteen years as Secretary Treasurer of the City. Left to right: Earl, Noreen Watson and Mayor Nazir Ahmad, March 28, 1983. (Reminder)

A field at Centoba Park was dedicated on April 25, 1983 in memory of Lloyd Wright, a long time member of the Lions Club. (Reminder)